Catch & Release

Other Books by Robert F. Wolff and Majestic Glory

UNITY: Awakening the One New Man

Have You Seen the Lamb?

My First 40 Days with the Lord

Sitting with Seamoor

Kingdom Calling: A Field Manual for Believers

Catch & Release

A Church Set Free

Robert F. Wolff

© Copyright 2015—Robert F. Wolff

All rights reserved. This book is protected by the copyright laws of the United States of America. This book may not be copied or reprinted for commercial gain or profit. The use of short quotations or occasional page copying for personal use is permitted and encouraged. Permission will be granted upon request. All rights reserved worldwide. Unless otherwise identified, Scripture quotations are from the New King James Version. Copyright © 1982 by Thomas Nelson, Inc. Used by permission. All rights reserved. Scripture quotations marked KJV are from the King James Version. Scripture quotations marked NIV are from THE HOLY BIBLE, NEW INTERNATIONAL VERSION®, NIV® Copyright © 1973, 1978, 1984, 2011 by Biblica, Inc.™ Used by permission. All rights reserved worldwide. Scripture quotations marked TLV are from the Tree of Life Bible by Messianic Jewish Family © Destiny Image Publishers, Inc. Used by permission. All rights reserved. All emphasis within Scripture is the author's own.

Drawbaugh Publishing Group
444 Allen Drive
Chambersburg, PA 17202

ISBN 13 TP: 978-1-941746-22-6
ISBN 13 eBook: 978-1-941746-23-3

For Worldwide Distribution, Printed in the United States

1 2 3 4 5 6 7 8 / 19 18 17 16 15

Fare Thee Well

I tread lightly with a manuscript that upon first sight appears to be critical of the Church. But the fact is that I love the Church.

Great men and women of faith have molded my life. My own walk of faith began with my family, who has preserved their Jewish roots in the soil of tradition. I am forever grateful for each of them for keeping me grounded in love. And then there is Amanda, The Boss. She lived out the Word of God—such a strong spirit and steadfast walk. This book is truly the fruit on her tree.

My list of influencers could never be complete. God has blessed me with men and women of vision on every corner of my life. I dedicate this work to everyone who has accepted and encouraged me to take the higher road, with the firm belief this ministry would touch the hearts of many. I extend special thanks to my precious family, to Benjamin DeLaine and Esther Rosenberg, and to Dean my publisher, whose actions speak louder than any words.

The responsibility for the Church to be the standard of righteousness has to be achieved with believers who understand the need to walk in freedom. Let's be encouraged to step into our roles as end-time apostles and prophets, leaders and teachers. May this work inspire the church to release the body to achieve its destiny.

Make way.

Endorsements

Robert Wolff is one of the most perceptive commentators on today's Church and the importance of its restoration and alignment with Israel, the Messianic Jewish community and its own cooperative unity. His evaluations are stellar and worth applying by all who want to see that glorious Church.

Daniel Juster
Founding President of Tikkun International
Founding President of Union of Messianic Jewish Congregations

Bob Wolff has a timely word for the church and a prophetic vision that he articulates in *Catch & Release* with clarity and purpose. Today's church is at a crucial turning point and in a book that is part protest wrapped up in hope, Bob is throwing his weight into helping it make the turn. A new paradigm is emerging that defines success in ministry less as a numbers game and more about human impact both individual and social. Bob brings Israel and God's Kingdom purposes together in a biblical restoration that is refreshing and powerful.

Peter Tsukahira
Co-founder, Pastor, Kehilat HaCarmel
(Carmel Congregation) Israel
CEO, Israel Crossroads Institute (IXI) Ltd.

Catch & Release is a beautifully balanced assemblage of Scripture and anecdote giving us the key for building a healthy church—UNITY. Not the passive unity as described by the world, but the fiery, world-changing unity walked out by Jesus and His early disciples. If you're a "Kingdom-minded" believer who is ready to bust through old church paradigms and bring the exploits of Jesus outside the four walls of the church and into the world, then this is the book for you.

Alisa Jordheim
Founding Director, Justice Society
Author, Made in the USA: The Sex Trafficking of America's Children

What would the church look like if we did things the way Jesus did? How would we disciple? How would we approach outreach? How would we help our community? During these tumultuous days many churches and pastors are looking for these answers. *Catch & Release: A Church Set Free* is a biblically based blueprint to guide the Church back on track to its leadership calling.

Mike Bickle
Founder and Director, International House of Prayer

There is a river whose streams shall make glad the city of God,
The holy place of the tabernacle of the Most High.
God is in the midst of her, she shall not be moved;
God shall help her, just at the break of dawn.
The nations raged, the kingdoms were moved;
He uttered His voice, the earth melted.
The Lord of hosts is with us;
The God of Jacob is our refuge. Selah

Psalm 46:4-7

Cargo Hold

Foreword	*xiii*
Drop Anchor! Fishers of Men	*xv*

Part I Prepping Our Nets 1
   Chapter 1   The River of Life   3
   Chapter 2   Alignment   15
   Chapter 3   The Elephant in the Tabernacle   33
   Chapter 4   Bagel Theology   55
   Chapter 5   Determining Your "Net" Worth   59

Part II Let's Go Fishing 61
   Chapter 6   Casting Off   63
   Chapter 7   Catching Fish   69
   Chapter 8   Discipling is a Contact Sport   77
   Chapter 9   How to Fish   85
   Chapter 10   There Will Be a Catch   101

Part III Going Deep 107
   Chapter 11   The Good Shepherd   109
   Chapter 12   Good Works, Good Boat, Good Crew   121
   Chapter 13   The Spirit of America   133
   Chapter 14   The Fivefold Ministry   151

Part IV Walking on Water   161
   Chapter 15 The Tipping Point   163
   Chapter 16 Selecting the Seven   173
   Chapter 17 Getting Out of the Boat   189
   Chapter 18 Here Comes the Bride   199

Weigh Anchor!   *207*
Noteworthy Ketches   *209*
Fishing   *218*

Foreword

Little did I know when the One New Man Conference came to Farmington, New Mexico, in December 2011 that my life would take a turn. For that event there was a declaration drawn up from the First Nations of America in support of Israel. After signing that document I had the privilege of leading a delegation of Navajos and friends, including Robert Wolff, to the Promised Land. We presented the declaration to members of The Knesset, Israel's government. That kindled a wonderful, newfound relationship between our First Nations and Israel.

Following our journey to Jerusalem we visited the Negev, the desert region in the southern part of the country. We were struck by the remarkable transformation we witnessed as this resourceful nation has turned their wilderness into a garden overflowing with abundant farmlands, vineyards, and agricultural projects. The following year four Israeli agricultural experts returned to our land to share their wisdom with our farmers.

We were greatly inspired as the First Nations of America share a similar vision of turning our own reservations into fruitful gardens. Thus began a profound social and spiritual journey that has enriched my own life, as well as others.

Since I started walking with God I have come to realize that different parts of the church seldom cooperate in outreach. This is not to say that the First Nations are not deeply grateful for the ministry and charity of those who have come alongside to meet our needs. In many ways churches have been our friends, but I wonder how long it will take for the church to truly grasp the vision of unity that Jesus taught.

I know it has been the grace of God that is leading the First Nations out of our stormy past of broken promises into a bright future built on cooperative commerce. The Lord is now calling our First Nations to be leaders in the critical days rapidly approaching.

It is my wish that this book would inspire many to walk as one. We are beginning to see what can happen when nations decide to bless one another. We need each other. This is a good place to start.

Ben Shelly
President of the Navajo Nation, 2011-2015

Drop Anchor!
Fishers of Men

*Then Jesus said to them, "Follow Me, and I will make you become **fishers of men**." They immediately left their nets and followed Him* (Mark 1:17-18).

The Eastern sky speckled pink in anticipation of dawn. Half an hour had lapsed since Dad had ruffled my locks. The spring on the screen door protested, surprising the rooster. In response, he twice bugled his morning report as we tiptoed across the front porch. I was up at the break of day, trusty rod in hand, tackle box clanging on my side with each step.

The pickup came to life, chugging across the cornfield, headlamps leading the way. The dew kept the dust to a minimum. Just a short hop past the bridge. Sworn to secrecy regarding the covert acquisition of a half-dozen glazed, strawberry jam-filled donuts. Mom would've had a hissy fit. Besides, anything that tasted that good couldn't be bad for me, especially on a frosty morning that made me weigh my sanity for leaving a warm, woolen blanket.

But once the sun rose to broadcast its radiant rays across the rippled river, everything made perfect sense. God certainly knew what He was doing when He taught us to fish.

Let's journey back in time down the River of Life to discover how our Lord approached His first followers. Let's take a close look at how Yeshua teaches His disciples to build the Kingdom of God. Let's see how He prepares them to become "fishers of men." Let's grasp how these future apostles learn to "catch" new believers. And let's examine the way Jesus instructs us to "release" these disciples back into the mainstream. Finally, let's explore what it takes to get out of the boat and walk on water! (No doubt you noticed that I used the names Yeshua and Jesus interchangeably in this paragraph, and have done so throughout the book. My reasoning is simple, Yeshua in Hebrew means "salvation"—who is Jesus Christ throughout the New Testament and the Messiah, prophesied throughout the Old Testament. Yeshua and Jesus are one in the same.)

The lovingkindness of our Lord is magnified through the good deeds of saints. Service is the place where the Kingdom of God makes contact with the world. We won't gain a full understanding of God's love without giving of ourselves. Likewise, we shouldn't expect the world to receive what God offers till they see us in action. Community service and missional outreach were never meant to replace prayer or praise; but neither should they be subordinated.

There is a process Jesus asks us to embrace for discipling. We are expected to follow it as we follow Him. Failing to do so has led Western culture to lose its bearings on the open seas. Without a healthy church to model appropriate behavior, the world is left to cast its own vision for the future. We can point at the foibles of society in an attempt to lay blame for the diminished influence the church holds today; nonetheless, the basic reasons behind the church's ailments are chiefly the result of internal inadequacies as opposed to external agendas. We have the blueprint for constructing the Kingdom; yet instead of following it, we insist on criticizing the rest of the church and the world.

What would happen if we did follow Him?

In so doing, we could shift imbalances, restore alignment, and refresh the church's vision. We would see a radiant church, teeming with schools of hatchlings. For all the challenges we face, as the world fails to produce its promised hope for the future, more and more fish get hungry for truth. Be encouraged. Prepare your nets. Our God's plans will always prevail.

Although this book may appear critical, my heart's desire is to identify issues that we can improve and to direct us to partner in the process. As we encounter our personal challenges here, it is to stimulate us to conquer them, not to embarrass or criticize. We have the opportunity to strengthen our King's body, and we need each other to accomplish this most worthy endeavor—to be fishers of men.

Part I

Prepping Our Nets

Chapter 1

The River of Life

Above the River

Picture yourself in a small aircraft flying above a large river. From your aerial viewpoint you observe innumerable ponds in a myriad of shapes and sizes straddling the watercourse up and down its length, as far as the eye can see. Each pond has an inlet and outlet to receive and return water to and from the river, which is their source.

Returning to earth, you step out along this riverbank. Upon closer inspection you notice the ponds contain fish. Each pond is fitted with irrigation dams to control the water flow. These dams are fitted with screens allowing fish to enter; however, most of the exit screens are shut. Some of these manmade bodies of water are crowded with fish; on the other hand, the population of many is sparse.

At the ingress to every pond stands a post with a large wooden sign, signifying its custodian. You quickly realize that each reservoir displays the name of a different group: Southern Baptist, Assemblies of God, Church of Christ, Catholic, Seventh Day Adventist, Calvary, Methodist, etc. You name it; you can find it. Every pond has its own identity, yet all draw water from the same river.

Each reservoir is custom designed to catch fish. Watchmen are stationed by the watergates next to the signs, coaxing fish to enter and enjoy their specialized ponds. Arrows on the signs signify unique designs for capturing their subjects.

Once admitted to the ponds, the fish are enrolled in "schools" where they study new ways of swimming. Ideally, the waters should flow freely in and out as the fish learn to swim together harmoniously. The silvery occupants discover how to "pool" resources to help one another. The new disciples feel safe in their new surroundings.

The ponds appear peaceful. Within each waterhole the fish seem to get along fine. Those ponds with the best circulation sport frolicking finned fishes. Shallow troughs run between pools from occasional floods and large rainstorms. At such times the fish are able to mingle and play as they celebrate the deluge. These big gatherings are short-lived as the fish are quick to return before the waters recede.

In the ponds where circulation is restricted, it's a dismal story. Their environment is murky. The water is not running and lacks depth. Many fish gulp air from above the surface, as their gills can't filter enough oxygen. It's not unusual for these fish to get so accustomed to the calm water, warm temperatures, and limited vision that they no longer seek a way out. They don't think much about the river.

Eventually the water becomes stagnant. An alarming number of waterholes have gone dry, even though the river is just a few meters away and easily accessible. Although many ponds suffer from similar afflictions, the watchmen don't pay much attention to anyone else's maladies. They don't talk much. After all, they have their hands full taking care of their own problems.

In those fortunate places where caretakers allow their fish to return to the river, an interesting phenomenon occurs. The moving waters in these reservoirs run clear. Upon release, the healthy swimmers go upstream to spawn. Many more fish can use the river. The whole ecosystem is improved.

This is a picture of the church in the United States of America.

> *When I returned, there, along the bank of the river,*
> *were very many trees on one side and the other.*
> *Then he said to me:*
> *"This water flows toward the eastern region,*
> *goes down into the valley, and enters the sea.*
> *When it reaches the sea, its waters are healed.*
> *And it shall be that every living thing that moves,*
> *wherever the rivers go, will live.*
> *There will be a very great multitude of fish,*
> *because these waters go there;*
> *for they will be healed,*
> *and everything will live wherever the river goes.*
> *It shall be that fishermen will stand by it*
> *from En Gedi to En Eglaim;*
> *they will be places for spreading their nets.*
> *Their fish will be of the same kinds*
> *as the fish of the Great Sea,*
> *exceedingly many."*
>
> Ezekiel 47:7-10

The Church

There are many fish swimming in the rivers that run by our churches that seldom come in contact with believers. Too many denominations have believed that their way of establishing Kingdom living is superior to others, so there is little effort to fellowship outside of their congregation. Even in the healthiest denominations there is very little sharing of resources with other parts of the body.

It's difficult getting pastors or churches together for anything. If we are able to connect and pray that's wonderful, but partnering in ministry is seldom even contemplated, much less discussed. Ongoing collaborative efforts are rarely accomplished.

If there is an evangelist or a Christian concert in the city, the church joins together, ever so briefly, then it's back to our individual groupings. Instead of putting fish back into the river of life we are creating separate ecosystems. Our problem is obvious. There is no biblical model for separate churches.

Somewhere along the line we decided that if we all worshiped and honored the same Lord that would be adequate to call ourselves united. We conveniently forget we are to be interwoven together into His body. To make matters worse, we are acting as if the other parts of His body aren't as good as our own.

We even quote First Corinthians 1:10-17 as we teach sectarianism is sin. We are operating as if our own pond is the center of the universe, so the condition of other ponds is of little concern. First Corinthians 12:25 says, *"there should be no schism in the body, but that the members should have the same care for one another."* We study, teach, and preach how the different parts of the body have to work together to be unified, but we know we are not successful.

From the air we can see that most of the ponds are losing their vitality. But when we are swimming in our own pond, we miss what God sees. Fewer than 10 percent of the major denominations are growing. The river of life is passing by the church that is supposed to be stocking it with fresh fish every season. Each spawning season we return fewer and fewer fish. We need to rediscover what it means to be "fishers of men" (referring to "men" collectively, without preference to gender or age).

The Fish Farm

John chapter 17 is known as the High Priestly Prayer of Jesus. The Lord has completed His work of ministry to His disciples. This is His prayer to God the Father. Knowing that He has fulfilled His calling, Yeshua now makes a request on behalf of all His followers. He asks God to have those who come to know Him as Messiah to have the same relationship with God that He has. Yeshua says:

> *"I have given them the glory that you gave me, that they may be one as we are one—I in them and you in me—so that they may be brought to complete unity. Then the world will know that you sent me and have loved them even as you have loved me"* (John 17:22-23 NIV).

Yeshua wants every one of His disciples to be one. Our identity is in Yeshua. He asks God to embrace us the same way He has embraced His Son. Why? So the world will see the unity of believers. That unity represents the full acceptance of God. This is a gift of immeasurable value. This is the pathway God has paved so the world would understand true love.

Without that unity the world will not know that God sent Yeshua, or that God loves us in the same fashion as He loves His very own Son! It's that important. Our witness to the world is gauged by our ability to walk together as "one new humanity."

A church that is not unified is a church that has redefined the love of God for its own purposes.

God does not want a divided church. When we "catch a fish" in our contemporary church world, our vision for discipling that new believer strays far from the avenue Yeshua lays out for us. This should give us pause and even some trepidation. A church that is not unified is a church that has redefined the love of God for its own purposes.

Where do we miss the mark? It's in the process of discipling.

When we bring new believers into our churches, we try to conform them into an image of our own making. If that is a denomination, then we must tread very carefully. We aren't just looking for new believers. We insist on having more Southern Baptists, more Methodists, more Episcopalians, and the list goes on. That is *not* what Yeshua asked for.

We think that fishing means to catch a wild salmon in a river, then place it in a pond marked with the name of our home assembly. We intend to raise that salmon and change it into another species. That species will only spawn young fry that have the look and image of our congregation.

These fish were born for the running rivers and swimming the seas. They will not be healthy inside a closed environment. The water putrefies. The diet is different. The natural process of growing and reproducing has been altered.

We act as if we are being faithful to our cause, but our cause puts branding above believing. Our cause has been relabeled and marketed to grow the size of our church. The health of the family of believers is measured by the love we have for one another. If our love is in God, and His love is in us, then the church will be unified.

If we want to know how healthy the church is, then we must look at our unity. If we truly are Yeshua's disciples, then the church will operate as a healthy body does. All of our bones will be properly aligned. We will walk upright in the spirit of lovingkindness. We will be a family joined in love as one body. We will support each other. A healthy church is a healthy family.

This is what Yeshua prayed for. This was His last prayer to His followers. Let's face it, we have not built the church He asked us to build.

> *And he has given us this command: Anyone who loves God must also love their brother and sister* (1 John 4:21 NIV).

So how do we get these fish back into the River of Life?

A Shrinking Church

A shrinking church is a sinking church. We are not asking ourselves why we are not keeping our heads above the water. In our self-centered piousness we choose not to notice the canary in the coalmine of Christian culture is not tweeting as loudly as our cell phones. Is it because we don't want to listen? Have we become so self-directed that, just as Peter's unsuccessful foray upon returning to the Sea of Galilee, we believe we know how to fish without seeking our Lord's advice?

God wants us to know His will and to follow Him. He has not made it difficult to do His bidding. This tells us that the genuine intimacy we have with Jesus offers us abundantly more than what we have perceived it to be. This new life is accessible. This is a life lived immersed in the river of God that is full and overflows with His presence. In this river, there is eternal life and supernatural buoyancy.

Assuredly, *"without faith it is impossible to please God"* (Hebrews 11:6 NIV). And without faith, no one walks on water. What does Jesus say to Peter as he takes his eyes off of his Master and starts to sink below the waves? *"O you of little faith, why did you doubt?"* (Matthew 14:31).

Let's takes a hard look at church culture. We have embraced and adopted way too many of the standards of the world around us. We should not be surprised that this has not sustained the growth of the church in the Western world. Fortunately, we still have the Word of God to point us in the right direction.

Please don't think of these comments as derogatory about the church. The church is our Lord's means to evangelize and save a sinking world, so condemnation will not gain our goal. Let's ask the questions that must be asked to provoke the church to the jealousy found in the first disciples. Along the way, we'll provide a few biblically founded insights. Certainly other questions must be asked, and other insights will be revealed as we learn about fishing for men.

Grab your shades, sandals, and sword. Prepare to launch your vessel. And let's go fishing.

Getting Off Track

When the church goes fishing for souls, it does so with the intended purpose of fulfilling the Great Commission from Matthew chapter 28. This step of obedience begins with the highest of callings—to lead an individual to salvation and eternal life by accepting Yeshua haMashiach (Jesus the Messiah) as Lord and Savior. The Word of God tells us, *"the gift of God is eternal life in Christ Jesus our Lord"* (Romans 6:23).

This soul-saving experience initiates a great celebration in the heavens. Back here on earth we also celebrate, encouraging a swift move to baptism—a deeply significant Kingdom spectacle in and of itself. We return to the water, becoming immersed and rising up to new life. We are reminded of our beginnings in the liquid home of our mother's womb, our release into breathing fresh air. All this is further symbolized by the resurrection of Yeshua, as He emerges from death into life.

Our family gets excited. Friends are intrigued. A new season begins. Life takes on deeper meaning. This really is good news. The honeymoon has begun and we're off to a great start.

> *Because we have endorsed self-centered techniques for discipling, we have demoted Yeshua's words of restoration into a diminished dimension of God's intention.*

But it is the next few steps, the process of nurturing new believers, where we get off track. In those churches that take the steps for discipling seriously, methods for building and equipping these "fresh fish" can take on some peculiar types of preparation. Because we have endorsed self-centered techniques for discipling, we have demoted Yeshua's words of restoration into a diminished dimension of God's intention. Sadly, too many churches are putting these new saints into ponds without giving proper consideration to our ultimate goal of returning them to the river.

This error is often the result of a hands-off versus a hands-on approach to discipling. Yeshua gave clearly mandated instructions to His followers that are contained in the Holy Scriptures. And we must delve into these sacred words to gather their meaning and apply them to our lives. We must study the Word of God to show ourselves approved by our King.

With the best of intentions, we train up our recently "caught" newborn in the ways of the Lord, that as they mature they would not depart from their faith. However, we must take care not to overemphasize internalizing the Word of God without the essential goal of "releasing" them to swim again in the River of Life. Once the arrow of our newfound faith has been prepared to strike its target, it is placed on the bow. As the tension is increased by the infilling of God's Word a formidable weapon is poised to be launched. The Holy Spirit reveals our calling and we are released to do His will.

By no means are we diminishing the value of a bedrock understanding of God's Holy Word. The Bible is our guidebook and blueprint for living. Without its foundation, we cannot build the Kingdom of Heaven. A wise saint will draw from its wells of wisdom every day. It is our anchor in the storm. The Word leads us beside still waters to rest in God. And it challenges us to look more closely at the pathway to biblical understanding to see where it directs us—to be doers, not just listeners.

> *Thy word is a lamp unto my feet, and a light unto my path* (Psalm 119:105 KJV).

The method of training prescribed by our King takes us out of the church courtyard and into the lives of broken, hungry people. And let's not assume that this requires a vow of poverty or celibacy. The whole earth is filled with God's glory and we are commissioned to go out and to carry the gospel to the whole world; to the high places as well as the low ones. A great many missionaries realize their lives may lack the recognition and sophistication we tend to seek for ourselves, but a life of service that reflects the heart of God is the most rewarding and edifying avenue to fulfillment. Yeshua is asking us to place glory above glamour. He wants to see souls become complete. He wants us healed, whole, and filled with unspeakable joy.

We need to make the world our church.

To live such a lifestyle means we have to reevaluate our value system. Coming to faith means leaving some things behind that once were esteemed. God wants us to take a fresh look at our relationships. He expects us to bring light into dark places. Like it or not, this means we need to expand our sphere of influence. We need to make the world our church. As we travel on His pathways, God will use the seed of faith that He has supplied to bring forth His harvest of souls.

Church is a place of refuge, best viewed as a temporary campsite where we are restored to wholeness and righteousness. An on-fire believer is a burning bush of passionate flames driving out darkness and broadcasting glory into the shadows. "I shall be released," must echo down seminary hallways. As one of the classic songs of our ancestors chimed, "Fish gotta swim, birds gotta fly." We gotta do what we were designed to do! A fulfilled human being has to witness. There's no substitute.

We were made to move. Faith is a stretching exercise. When we are taught the Word of God, we are filled with the knowledge of God. We have an unquenchable hunger for new, untrodden pastures to forage. The surge of enthusiasm that comes from knowing God cannot be quenched with passivity and complacency.

We have to face the truth that cannot be denied by dwindling memberships in the body. We are sacrificing the future of the entire church by telling our disciples that, "Our church is better than their church." Nor does migration to a "better church" where we're "better fed" alter the headcount in the army of God. Grabbing livestock from someone else's pasture seldom builds a healthier ranch.

Too many of our training pathways fail to accomplish their goal—to release a mature believer who is prepared to advance the Kingdom of God. Yeshua is looking for folks who want to strike out into Samaria, head into the urban jungles, and lay hands on the sick. Nothing less will do.

The outdoors classroom is essential. And what we learn there refines our precious metal and sharpens our steel to advance the Kingdom of God. Our passion has to be meshed with the hearts of others of like minds and callings. That is why Yeshua declares as He commissions, *"Go therefore and make disciples of all the nations…"* (Matthew 28:19).

Yeshua came to restore the Kingdom of God. He came to fulfill the calling that the Lord placed upon Abraham in Exodus 19:5-6—to make Israel a *"kingdom of priests and a holy nation,"* dedicated to God. God does more than offer salvation; He gives us a renewed passion for living. These new believers burn brightly with the light of Yeshua illuminating their very souls. And where passion is discovered, there is purpose and life becomes a fulfilling experience with eternal consequences.

There is no biblical model for building denominations. But that's what we've done, and that's where we continue to inappropriately apply our energies. The result is a divided church that struggles and competes against the other branches of the same tree meant for life. This tug of war for spiritual superiority is not befitting the body of believers. We are grafted together into one tree.

We have been divided for so long that we now wear our distinctiveness from other portions of Christ's body as a badge of honor. How many churches emphasize perceived deficiencies of other denominations as foundational building blocks to justify the supposed superiority of their own carefully constructed training programs?

Discipleship often focuses on this injurious justification in an effort to highlight weaknesses in other denominations. Here, in the act of teaching new believers about the strength of our own particular branch of the tree that represents spiritual Israel, we take a chain saw to the other limbs.

Building up a branch of the church does little to nourish the roots. The roots are designed to nourish the branch. Unless we are connected to the sustaining vine and design of Yeshua, we build His house in vain. Unless we are submitted to His Master Plan, we will not bear the fruit that lasts. Our purpose should *not* be equipping disciples for our community church; our ultimate goal is building up the saints to occupy places of authority in the Kingdom of God.

Chapter 2

Alignment

Dominion Is Ours

A new believer becomes part of the Kingdom of God—part of a grand design to oversee *every* aspect of life on planet Earth. Dominion is ours. This means education, commerce, social needs, and health, as well as spiritual growth.

Trying to build a local church into a mega-church may satisfy the needs of a particular group, but it falls well short of Kingdom-minded restoration. Building a mega-church can do much to advance the Kingdom. It's not the size of the church that is objectionable. It is what we do with the church, in how we build disciples, that requires an overhaul.

In our own minds we think we are building up the Kingdom of God by building up our own congregation. So we focus on church growth: more pews; larger offerings; bigger buildings, and the like. We seek to construct a self-contained church that fulfills every need of our congregation. We may try to justify this behavior under the guise of taking dominion. But this is an inappropriate application of this principle.

This model of a large church or synagogue dominating a city does not exist in the Holy Scriptures. This is why the Lord told

Samuel, when Israel insisted on their own king, that the people rejected God, not Samuel.

We want to be like everybody else, yet we are too shortsighted to recognize that competition restricts favor. We want to compete for favor. We want our king to be better than their king. Israel rejected God's design so they could be like the other nations. But God knew this would fail. It failed for Israel and it is failing for us too.

> *There is one body and one Spirit, just as you were called in one hope of your calling; one Lord, one faith, one baptism; one God and Father of all, who is above all, and through all, and in you all* (Ephesians 4:4-6).

A house divided is a church that will not grow or sustain itself in a world that increasingly rejects God and insists on its own kingship. A divided house of God will not hold up if it misinterprets secularism as its highest expression of freedom. A church that disciples new believers by emphasizing our differences separates one group of believers from another. That is division, not multiplication.

Building big churches may fulfill the vision of a genuinely anointed pastor, but does it fulfill God's master plan for salvation? Big churches can accomplish grand designs. There is nothing inherently wrong with a big church. Three times a year the Lord called all of Israel to worship as one.

The question that must be answered is whether the body is growing closer together or farther apart. A healthy body is well-coordinated. The parts, while each having their own function, work in unity. They recognize their common goal and assist all the other parts in fulfilling their highest calling—advancing the Kingdom as we glorify our King, who is the Head of the body.

When Pharaoh hands the keys to his empire to Joseph, it was not just to run his household. When Nebuchadnezzar put Daniel in charge, it wasn't just to be a priest for holy rites. These men were the overseers of every detail of life. That's God's Kingdom mindset.

Unless we, the church, begin to view salvation as entry into a vast network of anointed and appointed leaders to institute righteous rulership under God's direction, we put each of them into a small fishing boat with one pole and one handheld net, who will struggle to feed his own household.

God's economy is for His Kingdom to extend around the globe in new millennial ministry that so softens the hearts of believers that righteousness is a way of life, not a distant goal we hope to achieve after we die and enter the pearly gates.

Seldom does a church add new converts for the sake of advancing the Kingdom of God. Most likely, each denomination and congregation expand their population within the confines of their own culture. We are bumping into walls of our own making.

When we bring people to Yeshua, it's for His glory, not ours. If that's our motivation, then we can build a church of any size we want.

Navigating the Straight Line

The church of believers has been designated to bring forth the Kingdom of God here on earth. As members of our Lord's body, we recognize we have been formed to overcome darkness and bring forth His light. To reach that goal, our Lord prepares us for a journey. That pathway requires us to travel at God's speed. Since God travels at the speed of light, He is building an army that moves and operates at light speed. Thus, every obstacle toward this end must be removed.

The faith-based church is our Lord's vehicle to transform the world He created to become the community He destined us to be—one with Him and one with each other. God never expected us to do this without His guidance, vision, and gifts. That is why He sent His only begotten Son, Yeshua, to demonstrate that His power is here. His Holy Spirit remains to remind us that His presence will assist us to complete this calling. This can only be accomplished as His saints are appropriately aligned.

The only part of a vehicle that touches the road is its tires. Before we bolt tires to a car, they are methodically balanced and aligned. We all understand what happens when a vehicle is not carefully set up—as speed increases, improperly balanced and misaligned tires start to vibrate, causing dangerous instability. Correspondingly, when the Church is on target and navigating in a straight line, she will accomplish with speed and agility the awesome works God has destined for His Kingdom. To that end, significant adjustments must be made to achieve, restore, and maintain this stability wherever it is needed.

Apostle Peter was a leader. His role was to exemplify how to be effective, successful fishers. We shake our heads when we read of Peter's exploits to prove his loyalty to his teacher. Intuitively we know that Peter is no different from you and I. Yeshua had to show Peter that his enthusiasm was not enough to satisfy God's purposes. Peter had to reconfigure his priorities to become the disciple God had destined for him. To adequately accomplish this required direct confrontations. At the conclusion of His ministry on earth, the Lord asked Peter three times if he really loved Him.

To answer that query Peter had to grapple with his zealous tendency to control situations. This attitude had precipitated Peter's fervent claims to fearlessly defend the one who had laid down his life. Yeshua was now testing Peter's love. He had miserably failed his teacher, despite his insistence that such a predicament would never occur. The "big fisherman" had to humble himself and reassign his priorities to honor Yeshua's threefold request to feed His sheep through acts of lovingkindness. Simply casting nets, even with the best of intentions, was not enough. Fishing with Jesus takes a soft heart. Peter, like you and me, had to learn this lesson before he could teach it.

Paul encountered a similar recognition of spiritual authority as he was dumped onto his buttocks on his way to Damascus. God intervened out of His Majestic Glory and spoke to Paul, letting him know in no uncertain terms that his behavior was unacceptable. Paul had to be blinded to gain the necessary insight about honoring our Lord's decrees. Nothing less will satisfy our King.

As the primary author of the New Testament, Paul addresses significant reasons for the problems facing the emerging church. During that era, as first-born believers sought to attain a healthy balance and to walk uprightly, the early church had to learn how to follow our Lord's guidelines. The saints of God must master how to be fishers of men to effectively reach a pagan world. All of us need to assimilate our Patriarch's lessons.

Those freshly bred believers faced a world already steeped in competing doctrines from preexisting cultures and deeply entrenched belief systems. Recognizing humanity's stiff-necked resistance to God's design, while making this task more accessible to the newcomers of our faith, Yeshua likened evangelism to fishing. In so doing, Yeshua would give familiar context to apply those proven methods required to establish God's Kingdom.

During his travels, apostle Paul reiterated these principles to the freshly planted churches in an array of thriving metropolitan areas. His letters reflect his heartfelt partnership in the quest to anchor these fledging congregations to Yeshua's words in preparation for inevitable cultural clashes. Paul knows by virtue of his own religious history that each established spiritual hierarchy, with their longstanding traditions leaning on idolatrous beliefs, would challenge the message of faith in Yeshua. Most assuredly this would test the new doctrines espoused by this itinerant evangelist, who uncompromisingly claimed that Elohim sent His Son Yeshua, to be the Messiah of Israel.

The spiritual practices of the occupants in the cities surveyed in Paul's epistles were clearly out of sync with those called to follow in Yeshua's footsteps. Just as Peter, Paul, and the disciples discovered firsthand how well the principles necessary to be fishers of men worked in the mission field outside of Israel. The very veracity and effectiveness of first century Christian theology was beginning to impact the world's great cultural and trade centers. Apostle Paul's burden was to assure these newcomers that Yeshua's principles, when put to practice, would thrive and keep these churches properly aligned in even the most hostile environments.

For the Kingdom of God to advance, it had to confront and conquer these dissenting voices. Paul accomplished this by teaching believers how to be acceptably attuned and in proper accord with God and each other. The Letter to the Church in Ephesus reflects the apostle's divinely guided instructions for equipping saints for the work of ministry. This describes how the church prepared for service in the first century. The lessons once learned during those dynamic days need to be resurrected to activate similar strategies for our contemporary church.

Early in this epistle, Paul points out our calling to the Kingdom of God as he unveils our identity as one new man. As we uncover God's plans for salvation, this mystery of our true identity is revealed. He goes on to prescribe our armor for overcoming principalities, powers, rulers of darkness, and hosts of wickedness. Such groundbreaking statements surely invigorated the population of that city. Paul details and directs these emerging outposts of faith into divinely ordained combat-ready outreaches characterized through humble service. The missional outreach church was being shaped.

Peter and Paul were learning how to fish according to God's design. In turn, the Lord placed them into particular circumstances that allowed them to share the lessons they had learned directly from Kingdom authority. That process has not changed since its inception. More importantly, it worked then; and it does now.

The explosive expansion of the church during that era speaks volumes regarding the benefits of employing God's plan for salvation and education of new believers. The church that is capable of catching fish is best suited to teach others how to bring in a tremendous haul themselves. Sharing these techniques gains favorable results that are the "catch" from being properly aligned and mastering navigation on the open seas.

Paul caught a lot of "fish" in these distant regions. This model was used to carry the good news to the Gentiles, as well as Jews. Employing these carefully constructed godly principles for targeted, hands-on discipling results in a revived and reawakened church capable of navigating deep waters as it lands a net-busting haul, teeming with fish.

Equipping

First, Paul lays out the guidelines for Kingdom authority, complete with offices, titles, and a vision for walking out one's faith. The apostle shows us the purposes for God's gifts. Focusing on Ephesians 4:11-16, we encounter the blueprint for establishing a healthy church. Five offices are mentioned to accomplish this goal: apostle, prophet, evangelist, pastor, and teacher.

The last two offices are often coupled together. For our discussion we will keep these slots separate. There are obviously individuals who appear to display more than one assignment and that's certainly within the realm of possibility. But our goal here is to unpack the function for these positions of spiritual authority. In that light, even if there are overlapping mantles, we can still differentiate the reasons for the offices. Later on, we will discuss the specific callings for each of the offices.

When we study the Greek term Paul used for equipping in Ephesians 4:11, *katartismos,* we discover that one of its uses refers to mending and repairing, such as setting a broken bone into the correct position; another definition is to recover your right mind or to restore appropriate thinking. Paul expounds on how those in leadership need to prepare the body to perform its proper functionality. He shows us the divine plan for equipping God's people by building up new disciples—in other words, how to get aligned.

Paul's imagery for alignment describes a well-balanced, smoothly functioning human body. Starting with the Head, which is Yeshua, each part has a necessary activity that allows the entire persona to move in the grace and freedom prescribed by God. Paul describes this divine response as the whole body, not just individuals. This includes every aspect of the Kingdom: churches, ministries, missions, and outreach. To be set in proper order, every part of the body needs to be joined together, unified.

The first cousin of that term is *katartizo*. This also speaks of setting things in order; more specifically to make fully ready, to repair, and prepare. This is the word used in Matthew 4:21 to describe James and John's actions as they were mending their nets in their father's boat the day Yeshua called them out to follow Him and learn God's way of fishing. Some translations use the terms ligament or connector.

The church claims to respond to these terms in principle. We say the body is balanced and aligned. Pastors preach unity. Teachers teach unity. But we don't reach unity. So we have to ask ourselves why we agree in principle, but not in practice.

Just as a laser beam works by concentrating energy into a narrow shaft of light that shoots across the heavens, a body that is perfectly positioned has the ability to stretch across vast distances to bring God's glory to faraway places. When we are aligned to be Yahweh's agents of transformation, nothing is out of reach.

Our goal then, is to set the body straight. We need to align broken limbs. And we need to restore proper thinking. To accomplish these tasks we must calibrate the body of God's Kingdom to be perfectly aligned with the cornerstone, which is Yeshua, and to be perfectly plumbed to raise up the body's structure, which houses the dwelling place of God.

There is a functionality of purpose woven into the fabric of the Kingdom of God. The focus is not upon titles, but upon equipping the saints for works of service. If you will, the Lord is about building a Kingdom that equips the Church culture to recognize and rectify the basic needs of each community. The self-serving image of power-hungry leadership must be shed for our new garments so that we would be clothed in Christ, who chose to step away from His royal place in Heaven, to set aside His standing with God, to come near, and to serve here.

The result of weaving this new creation produces a soft, loving fabric that touches and soothes our broken world. This is not just a feel good phenomenon. The composition of a life following salvation initiates an internal transformation. Such a person is marked by lovingkindness and mercy. Unlike corporate models of power and prestige, the most highly valued and attractive attire of those called to leadership in God's superstructure is humility.

Such a response, to become the clay in the hands of a holy God, only occurs after an individual has accepted God's calling. Alignment must come as an act of our free will. We must choose our pathway. God lays out the way, but the choice is ours. Humility only comes by submission; our free will must be involved. Freedom may be won through much turmoil, but it has no value if we are deprived of our relationship with God. When our choice is to put God above all things, our body will align to His calling and we will do mighty deeds that glorify the One who is our peace.

This new identity given to us by God is both internal and external. Salvation is an all-encompassing event. In its wake we are driven to demonstrate the transformed life of one who has had an encounter with the living God. Nothing can or will ever be the same. We are assured of a caring, compassionate, loving, and everlasting relationship with the Lord of Heaven and earth. That's what makes us humble. It is only natural that we would want to share this relationship with all we encounter.

This mission to touch the world with God's heart defines our walk—it pushes the blood through our veins. Humility is our clothing and love is our purpose. Compassion motivates our calling. The ability to give and receive lovingkindness is the quality that identifies a mature believer, driving us to make a difference every day. Even when circumstances display danger, compassion tells us that we must press on toward the highest calling—to serve God and humanity with lovingkindness. Compassion swings the compass of humility and directs our paths toward righteousness.

On this high pathway, even suffering for Christ becomes a privilege. The pain of persecution pales in comparison to avoiding a witness of God's truth. God's mercy uncloaks evil intentions, exposing the irrational quest for power that only rules through fear. In stark contrast to the grinding destruction of invading darkness, a fearless believer moves with a flowing symmetry.

The analogy of a well-balanced, smoothly moving anatomy is displayed so all can see how the corporate body of the church operates. We follow the Head, which is our Lord, who directs all of our activities. Without a clear understanding of the rule of our King, the body will not perform the tasks for which it was designed. It will flail about like a fish out of water with little or no attention paid to higher purposes.

The main goal of a body without alignment is satisfying the flesh. For a while this seems enjoyable. But short-term ambitions leave us empty, with no lasting contribution for upcoming generations to benefit by or build upon. Heaven forbid our legacy is defined by people blindly tweeting out extraneous texts to the tune of egocentric footsteps. This is not a condemnation of social media; it's a comment on how the next generation has decided to use an incredibly powerful means of communicating with their peers. We have reduced our uses of technology to ingenious means of expressing our self-centered need for status. What for? To prove our worth? God's love comes gratis, not by status.

God's love comes gratis, not by status.

A body aligned under God's calling is compassionate, humble, and willing. This is the appearance of a mature saint. This is a person who wants to change the world for its highest purpose. This is the picture Paul shows us of leadership in Ephesus constructing a legacy of love. This is how an individual becomes balanced and aligned. It is a vision to be emulated and esteemed by the rest of the body, inspiring us for the work of the ministry.

> *For the perfecting of the saints,* ***for the work of the ministry,*** *for the edifying of the body of Christ:* ***till we all come in the unity of the faith,*** *and the knowledge of the Son of God, unto a perfect man, unto the measure of the stature of the fulness of Christ* (Ephesians 4:12-13 KJV).

There it is in black and white: ***"till we all come in the unity of the faith."*** The Lord is showing us how to become united. It won't come through religious debates or through humanity's models for success. A working world will come through *"the work of the ministry"*—good works. The method that yields fruit is the one the God has sent to us through His Son.

Tearing Down Babel

At the Tower of Babel, God confounded our language. Why? Humanity was building a massive structure that reflected our own abilities, not God's.

> *Then they said, "Come, let us build ourselves a city, with a tower that reaches to the heavens, so that we may make a name for ourselves; otherwise we will be scattered over the face of the whole earth"* (Genesis 11:4 NIV).

In His mercy, God responded to humankind's first declaration of independence to *"build ourselves a city,"* by doing exactly what we had tried so hard to avoid—He scattered us. Constructing or designing projects that fail to honor our proper relationship with God is vanity. On the surface, such behavior may appear to be righteous, but in truth it offends our Maker. The Lord's response to this effort was to confuse us by confounding our language, then to disperse us to the four corners of the earth. There we would remain to rebuild our lives for thousands of years.

On the day of Pentecost, the Lord reversed that curse and released His Holy Spirit to rectify the rift in our relationship. On that day a multitude of Jews were gathered in Jerusalem to celebrate Shavuot, God's giving of the Torah to Moses on Mount Sinai. Shavuot follows fifty days after Passover. It is one of three annual feast days when all devout Hebrew men were instructed to come to the Temple Mount.

Jerusalem was crowded. The previous time faithful Jews gathered in town was to celebrate Passover and Israel's exodus from Egypt.

At that time they had witnessed the crucifixion and resurrection of Yeshua. Now, fifty days later, as the Holy Spirit was being poured out on the City of David, participants from a multitude of foreign nations were hearing the gospel preached. What's more, these messages were being delivered in their native tongues from native Israelis, who were not familiar with these languages.

God spoke the world into existence, giving humankind one language. When we tried to imitate this feat by building the Tower at Babel, we were halted. We started with a common language, but got haughty. Thus we were given new languages that separated us. On Pentecost, coinciding with the celebration of Shavuot, God bridged this divide by using His disciples to speak in languages only known to foreigners.

The Lord showed us He would not honor our selfish behavior. Human history proves we will continue to repeat this error of self-reliance time and time again. For all the lessons we need to learn, our most tragic error comes from not recognizing the nature of our relationship with God. This leads to the most disappointing sagas driven by our own self-righteousness. We refuse to acknowledge that our actions repeatedly result in the same outcomes as we repeat the same errors. This is foolishness.

However, when we, His children, unite under His banner of lovingkindness, God will release His power and authority to change the world. Just as our disobedience yields failure, righteousness produces blessings. God promised us that He would honor our obedience. Ever since the first day of creation, His promises have always been fulfilled.

How much has changed since those days in Babel? We speak of unity, yet we are not united. The Lord has scattered us, albeit with the intent to reunite us. But, we the church resist unification. The body of Messiah seldom even tries to unite. After 2,000 years of growth, the church has spread around most of the earth. Yes, the church is ubiquitous—but disjointed, lacking a unified identity or vision. We tentatively hope if all claim to honor the same Messiah that will be sufficient to demonstrate our unity.

The voice of prophets reaches across time and the blood of martyrs stains the earth, but humanity still insists on its own ways. The church cannot move forward without grasping its call to righteousness. Much of what we call church has little spiritual vitality. But God has commissioned and stationed His "called-out" ones across the land. He has peppered the church with saints who want to encounter the living God. They are sitting next to you in the pews and singing beside you in the choir, preparing their nets. God is encouraging us to grab hands and become the ligaments needed to join together.

Once we recognize the issues at hand and come humbly before the Lord our God our Maker, He will bring forth the fires of Pentecost on such a scale that it shall eclipse every other move of God throughout world history. This will only be accomplished His way, not ours. When the revival kicks into gear, we are going to need a vast fleet of ships and a lot of folks who know how to catch and release fish.

Avoiding Labels

When inquiry is made as to our faith, saying, "I follows Jesus" or "I'm a child of God" seems inadequate. Normally we retreat to using the name of whatever house of worship appears over the door of our congregation as our answer. Failing to declare our identity in Yeshua Himself means we are carving out space for ourselves that the Lord doesn't want us to occupy.

The term "denominate" refers to the process of selection by dividing or partitioning into groups, sections, categories, or sects. The primary and most common use of the word "denominational" is for identifying different religious organizations such as Lutheran, Anglican, Episcopal, etc.

Humankind's history of subdividing the house of God gives precedence to a denominational identity that simply can't be found in the Holy Scriptures. We are more intent on splitting the flock to entice some dissatisfied sheep to join our band of believers than to lay down our differences and collectively contend against the spiritual forces of darkness. Ultimately it will be the unsaved who suffer the most as we in the church debate which fishermen have the best ship in the fleet. In the meantime, multitudes of lost souls descend to Davy Jones' Locker.

For all that believers have in common, there remain core issues we choose to ignore. The primary problem stems from our identity inside the body of Yeshua. We are inadvertently using titles and denominational labels that highlight the very same issues that divide and separate us from the rest of Christ's body. Even referring to our fellowship as "nondenominational" can be reactionary. Let's proclaim who we are. We are children of the Most High God!

For churches that don't want to be affiliated with an established group, the tendency is to strike out on our own. That decision seems good for a while. But while we avoid being pigeonholed by denominations, we also open ourselves up for attack due to the lack of mature elders in the faith who have learned how to hold us accountable. Running a church without the counsel of seasoned vets is asking for trouble. Instead of moving together in grace-filled symmetry, we emerge afflicted by Jacob's limp, which was caused by his insistence that God's angel do things his way.

Such competitiveness has left us vulnerable to cultish religious movements and church politics that revolve around personalities lacking sound, grounded theology. These organizations swiftly arise and fester due to the spiritual vacuum left by a fragmented body of believers. We see this as the "Post-Protestant" church shrinks in numbers and social standing. It is not good for man to be alone, anymore than it is for the church to be a house divided.

Before a lot of people go off in a huff and point to all the good his or her denomination has accomplished, know that most of us, including myself, have spent virtually all of our decades of time in the Kingdom as members and/or participants in a variety of denominations. I continue to attend a denominational church and enjoy my time there. Denominations accomplish great deeds and their roles are mostly beneficial. Mostly.

We maintain we have good reason for our differences, but that is not what our Lord prayed for. These walls must be torn down before Yeshua returns. It's not that we should be against denominations, it's that we are supposed to be for unity. And whatever stands in the way of unity must be reevaluated. There are no favorites at the foot of the cross, only favored. The power of the first century church was released into a unified body. Are we willing to sacrifice our sacred cows for the sake of the unity that defines the Kingdom of God?

> *There are no favorites at the foot of the cross, only favored.*

It is a sad testimony that the process of splintering the body of the Messiah has been rationalized through theological subdivision. There are ample biblical verses and theologies that point us toward unity. Yet it seems we are determined to build "unity" through some other means—notwithstanding the fact that this goal has eluded us for two millennia. Unsurprisingly, during these end times the same forces that want to tear down our cathedrals will also provoke us to reconstruct a far more unified body, notwithstanding our heretofore-estranged relatives. Soon and very soon, the prophecies of Romans chapter 11 will be fulfilled.

God asks us to pray for things to be on earth as they are in Heaven. Well, we all know that there will be one body in heaven. I'm not calling for the ending of denominations or associations. Please don't hear that. I'm asking for us to join our hearts, our hands, and our feet together in ministry. Seriously, this isn't tough to do.

We are often reminded of the high priestly prayer of Yeshua that we all would be one. John chapter 17 is often quoted, as this plea reflects Yeshua's final message before His death, through which He hoped to galvanize the fledgling church. The Lord knew that we would be highly susceptible to doctrinal differences. Paul's epistles continue this theme as they incisively warn us of inharmonious hazards.

We must constantly remind ourselves that Yeshua's dying declaration was for unity. Key passages of Scripture point to the final words before a prophet or ruler "breathes his last." For a believer, our last breath is all that separates us from being with our Lord. Yet Paul exhorts us, *"to live is Christ, and to die is gain"* (Philippians 1:21). Our call is to do our Lord's bidding now. Effective ministry today is the best way to ensure our eternal retirement plan is appropriately activated.

The Lord counseled us to establish His Kingdom on earth, as it is in Heaven. That Kingdom is unified. It is one; *"Hear, O Israel: The Lord our God, the Lord is one!"* (Deuteronomy 6:4). Oneness is unity personified. The Lord prayed for this to occur here and now.

For us to complete the work our Lord set before us, we have been instructed by Him to become one. We are not going to receive the full release of His power until we cross this chasm.

Have we failed to recognize that building a church that is a tower unto itself is the same error humanity made at Babel? Without proper understanding of how God wants us to build His Kingdom, we mistakenly claim the work of our hands is actually the work of God's hands. This is a dangerous miscalculation.

Yeshua is looking for a bride, not brides. He's not coming until we are ready. And we won't be ready until we are One in Him. That will only occur as we become One in each other. Mark the gospel writer tells us more:

> *One of the Torah scholars came and heard them debating.*
> *Seeing that Yeshua had answered them well, he asked Him,*
> *"Which commandment is first of all?" Yeshua answered,*
> *"The first is, 'Shema Yisrael, Adonai Eloheinu, Adonai Echad.'*
> *Hear, O Israel, The Lord our God, the Lord is one.*
> *And you shall love Adonai your God with all your heart,*
> *and with all your soul, and with all your mind, and*
> *with all your strength.*

The second is this: 'You shall love your neighbor as yourself.'
There is no commandment greater than these."
"Well said, teacher," the Torah scholar said to Him.
"You have spoken the truth, that He is Echad and besides Him
there is no other.
And to love him with all the heart, with all the understanding
and with all the strength, and to love the neighbor as yourself
is much more than all burnt offerings and sacrifices."
When Yeshua saw that he had answered wisely, He said to him,
"You are not far from the kingdom of God."
And no one dared any longer to question Him

(Mark 12:28-34 TLV).

The people who heard Yeshua speak these words no longer questioned Him. Let's pray that our legacy in the church is to follow Him and end divisive behavior. Yeshua is not looking for a better bride; He just wants a beautiful bride.

Chapter 3

The Elephant in the Tabernacle

Looking at the church, our lack of unity has made us easy pickings for our foe. We know we have this problem, but we choose to ignore its cause and look the other way. This is the elephant in the center of the tabernacle. Let's have the courage to begin this dialogue and wrestle with the real causes.

Our Lord knew the trials we would face. On the night before Jesus was crucified, John records our Messiah calling out to His Father, *"that they may be one just as We are one"* as He prayed for *"complete unity"* (John 17:22-23). This is our Lord's final heart cry to God Almighty before going to Gethsemane. This is the capstone of Yeshua's ministry on earth, as it is in Heaven.

Nevertheless, we have not fulfilled this essential calling to unity. We must not and cannot ignore this mandate. This is the key that releases the supernatural power of God in our midst. Our Lord instructs us that there is *"one flock and one shepherd"* (John 10:16). He says this because He knows this is the relationship we must honor with God and with each other for Him to act!

Granted, there are wondrous times when we join together. Our unity is best exhibited during times of evangelical outreach—Reinhard Bonnke comes to town, Promise Keepers calls out the men of God, Aglow International hosts a conference, or Michael W. Smith has a concert. These are holy convocations and invaluable gatherings of the saints. Here unity is most obvious, coming naturally as well as supernaturally, as we all join as one in Messiah.

So what's missing? Our *identity* in Yeshua! Without grasping who we are in the Messiah, we will not be the body of believers joined together as one, for which our Lord implored at the Last Supper. Going to church or worshipping with other believers does *not* establish one's identity or lead to the unity for which Yeshua prayed in John chapter 17.

Day-to-day life in the Spirit marches to a vast array of different drummers. Each ministry exhibits its own personality. This diversity within the body of believers yields a variety of expressions in outreach, each tailored to impact the surrounding community. However, unity is not about sameness, nor is it limited to diversity. Unity is inclusive—as we *"do good to all, especially to those who are of the household of faith"* (Galatians 6:10). It will be our ministry that makes us one; far more than our home assembly.

To be one in Yeshua is to focus on our identity in both Him as the Head, and fellow believers as His body. That identity rests in God's love. Our Father's love for us urges us to love Him and each other. Yeshua proclaims this love after one of the scribes asks, *"Which is the first commandment of all?"* (Mark 12:28). There is absolutely no doubt that God raises a standard and levels the playing field when it comes to love: *"Jesus answered him, 'The first of all the commandments is: "Hear, O Israel, the Lord our God, the Lord is one"'"* (Mark 12:29).

Love is how we identify ourselves and is inexorably tied to the measure of our faith. When we fail to connect to the church across the street, thereby truly living as God's family, we isolate ourselves from each other. This is how God asks us to build His Kingdom—on a foundation of love. This is how we grow.

We only fool ourselves when what we call "church growth" can be nothing more than "stealing livestock" from another church that desperately needs our prayer and support. The inevitable result is a power failure because we are not aligned with God's design for His church.

We have been operating from isolated positions for far too long. And contrary to our calling, we've settled for a divided state where we glorify Yeshua, the Head of the body, but won't lift a finger to help the rest of His body. A healthy congregation needs the other parts of the body. How else can we lift someone up when they fall? God gave us His gifts to share.

There is no substitute for unity. The best way to edify and join the body as one is to equip each believer for service. The fruit of our labors won't last if each successive generation is not released to their ministry calling. For the body to be robust, its ligaments must be joined together so that it can move and breathe and have its being in service to both God and humanity.

Keeping Unity

Ephesians 4:3 directs us how to walk in love by *"endeavoring to **keep the unity** of the Spirit in the bond of peace,"* and Paul lays it out clearly and succinctly in verses 4 through 6, cited previously.

If there are any questions about God's plan for unity, John 17:20-23 (TLV) gives us Jesus' high priestly prayer:

> *I pray not on behalf of these only, but also for those who believe in Me through their message, that they all may be one. Just as You, Father, are in Me and I am in You, so also may they be one in Us, so the world may believe that You sent Me. The glory that You have given to Me I have given to them, that they may be one just as We are one—I in them and You in Me—that they may be **perfected in unity**, so that the world may know that You sent Me and loved them as You loved Me.*

This is our Lord's last prayer before going to Gethsemane and the cross.

First Corinthians 1:10 (NIV) instructs us, *"that you **be perfectly united** in mind and thought."* No one can deny the necessity for unity is paramount in God's design. Yet every week we continue to divide that which the Lord tells us not to separate.

Who will win this battle of wills? Man or God? If you are siding with God, then you will win. If you are siding with God, you will also bump headlong into humanly established lines of authority in the faith-based community.

Now before you conclude this is a full frontal attack on denominationalism, this problem has not been caused by denominations. This type of division within the body is not causal, but rather symptomatic of the disease that paralyzes the expansion of the gospel.

Denominations came about because of disagreement about doctrine. And there is a necessity for doctrine. Some of the church's greatest advances have come by advancing sound doctrine. Sound doctrine builds a sound body. We are told to disciple the saints by declaring the whole counsel of God. Such instruction opens the Holy Scriptures for all to discuss and review. Doctrine is the proving ground for faith. Healthy debate over doctrine is enjoyable and informative. Doctrine is often our method for discovering the validity of our faith.

However doctrine is not eminent for a walk of faith. When the interpretation of God's Word takes us past the brink of cohesiveness within the body of our Lord, then the differing parts of the body of believers cease to operate in unison.

Consider communion. Communion means the act of coming together. This reflects both our relationship with God and with each other. Yet communion is one of the more divisive issues in the church. The interpretation of Jesus' request at the Last Supper to *"do this in remembrance of Me"* (Luke 22:19) has splintered the church and fed the movement toward denominationalism. Our enemy must chuckle over this predicament. Yeshua taught us that communion made us one in Him. Paul wrote: *"I urge you, brothers and sisters, to watch out for those who cause divisions and put obstacles in your way that are contrary to the teaching you have learned"* (Romans 16:17).

Is it healthy to air our views about communion? Of course! Will we have differing opinions? Of course! Should this cause division in the body? Of course not! Yet, as I mention an issue that may lead us to disagreement, consider the outcome if our debate leads to an argument. Can't we hear Jesus challenge the scribes and the Pharisees, *"He who is without sin among you, let him throw a stone at her first"* (John 8:7). Ever since that confrontation, Jesus still writes in the earth, awaiting our reply; watching for our response.

Are we not as quick to judge one another? Haven't we allowed such condemnation to determine the nature of our relationships in the church? Isn't this where enmity comes from? And hasn't Jesus broken down the wall of separation between us?

Yet we will defend our partisan positions, even unto death by stoning, which forces the church to divide and the three-strand cord to unravel, all in the name of righteousness. I must suggest that such an attitude is man's rightness, not the righteousness of God.

We don't have to agree on each of the interpretations of the Bible in order to be one in Jesus. This type of thinking does not build unity. Quite the opposite, our insistence on our own correctness denies the healing balm of God's righteousness.

God designed humanity with needs. These needs confirm and require the necessity of harmony with others to survive. We maintain harmony by accepting others who disagree with us. This is a measure of our love. Every relationship tests our ability to forgive. In forgiveness we recognize God's atonement for our sins.

We have gone so far as to alter Kingdom living into groups of exclusive clubs. Membership is defined by separation and insists on isolation from the rest of the body. What happened to the communion of love that accepts all things?

We pray that the world will repent and to come to salvation. Repentance is more than turning from sin. It is a change in the pattern of our thoughts. To repent means to take a fresh look and to offer unbiased review—to see with new eyes, and to hear with new ears. So if there is a challenge, it must be answered within the Word of God. Our identity comes from our King Yeshua, who is the Head of the church, not from the body.

The body's purpose is to do good works that glorify the Head, that is Messiah, not our own ministry. As long as we concentrate on church growth programs that are focused on the needs of the community (both faith-based and secular) there is no reason for the body to be divided. That's right, we reach out before we reach in.

Ephesians 4 takes us there. Within this chapter, the Lord shows us how to unify the body. Remarkably few have noticed God's prescription for unity in verse 12.

One fatal failure comes with our decision to take our identity from a denomination. When asked, "What is your faith?" Our reply is something like: "Southern Baptist," or "Methodist," or the like. We ignore Paul's warning about divisions.

So where have we missed the mark? By failing to show our love through acts and service of good works that transcend the divisions inside the church. I expect most will respond to this remark by reminding ourselves of the good things we have done to build the church. May I remind you that the church belongs to Him, not to us. Humility demands that we get past ourselves and look to God's commandments.

Love is the glue that holds this whole universe together. If we are not loving our fellow brothers and sisters as much as we love God, we have missed the boat.

And before you tell me that you understand love, you better tell me that your church is involved with other churches in ministry. If we can't demonstrate that bedrock requirement about love, we've missed the love boat.

> *"Why are we not conquering the obvious divisions within the church body, which God insists that we honor?"*

There is a long list of things churches do for their community, but how many churches partner with other parts of the faith-based community in service? That's where the rubber hits the road. (For a good example of meeting community needs, see *Neighborhood Initiative* in the Noteworthy Ketches section in the back of the book.)

So I must ask the obvious question, "Why are we not conquering the obvious divisions within the church body, which God insists that we honor?"

Not only is the answer to this question crucial, I believe our response is a prerequisite to our Lord's return. I must repeat this. I don't believe Jesus will come for His bride until His church operates in the fashion He has prescribed—that we be one!

For this reason, the church needs to consider what it means to be one new man. If we are going to live by the Spirit, then we need to walk in the Spirit—the Spirit of Love.

Light and Darkness

Light and darkness are not compatible. The church is God's gift to humanity as the vessel through which He may exhibit His light to His creation. The church is His vehicle to love His people, and no other plans of man can or will substitute. Love conquers all. It always has and it always will.

The darker the forces of evil, the brighter the light of the gospel shines. The power of love is unquenchable. Darkness knows no boundaries. But unlike love that radiates and emits light, darkness ultimately turns against itself. Because darkness is never satisfied, there is never enough of anything to satisfy its hunger or quench its evil thirst.

God brings light and peace. Darkness and fear may be used to control people, but they fail to bring love and peace. This is God's divine plan for showing us His glory—through His light. No plot of our foe can be successful or sustained, no matter how well-executed.

"There is no wisdom, no insight, no plan that can succeed against the Lord" (Proverbs 21:30 NIV).

Darkness is not the opposite of light. Darkness is the *absence* of light. Darkness is a place where light is yet to shine. Darkness has no power over light. Darkness does not understand light. Darkness tries to masquerade as if it offers some type of illumination. But once the true light appears, the differences between real light and counterfeit claims are easily distinguished.

Because we are all made in the image of God, we all will recognize God when we see Him. The only question is whether we genuinely hunger for our Creator, or if we have decided to create someone or something to take His place.

To die for a cause that exalts life glorifies God. To die for a cause that exalts death cannot honor our God who has given us life. Death that causes selfish destruction and shame brings no glory and no light. Others who live in darkness may rejoice in a death that robs others of life, but it does not lead to a place of eternal joy. Darkness is against all laws—spiritual, natural, and metaphysical.

There is no honor in doom, joy in destruction, or peace in fear. Because people respond so dramatically to darkness, our adversary uses it to control people. But when the true light shines, darkness flees.

What good does it do to "catch" a fish by revealing the light of our Lord Yeshua, then never "release" him back to the watercourse to share his testimony?

Love Levels the Landscape

To follow Yeshua is to follow what He commands. His commandment to love requires *both* loving God and loving each other. The love for each other is not a diminished or secondary type of love. Our love for each other is the actual demonstration and proof of how much we love God! The Lord tells us that we cannot claim to love God if we do not love one another. Fellowship with God is reflected in our love for our neighbors.

When asked about how we are to recognize the life of a believer, the response is clear—by our love. Of course people will want to know how much we love God. However, the real standard for measuring our walk with the Lord comes when the world sees how much care we exhibit regarding our fellow human beings, especially the ones with whom we strongly disagree! True love requires laying down our own agenda and picking up God's.

It costs far more than money to help people in need. Real love tests our resolve. Godly love undoes our self-image. It rearranges our priorities. It humbles us. Love isn't acceptable when we claim superior understanding or intellect. Love is best exhibited when we decide God's ways are better than our own. This is the love that requires temperance, not temerity. Love levels the landscape.

Today's church suffers from growing pains. These aren't the type from growing too fast; these are the pains that come from disobedience, causing the Lord to wait patiently for our submission to Him. A mature church knows how to love God, love our fellow members, and love others in our community. That's how God loves us. How can we call ourselves "godly" and not love the way God loves?

The Lord is not unwilling or reluctant to bless His family. He has given us guidelines that He expects us to follow to receive His promises. We claim to be waiting on God to bring us to the next level of life in the Spirit. Unfortunately, we are missing the fishing boat that the Lord has outfitted for us to spread the gospel. In fact, it is the Lord who is waiting on us! And we act as if we have performed as He has instructed us. We scratch our heads and complain that God is taking too long. We pray for God to move. But God's already right where He needs to be.

> *We pray for God to move. But God's already right where He needs to be.*

A good test for the health of the church is our love for the faith community. Unity is the outward vestige of our inner love for one another. This is how we observe the health of any family. Signs of strife and strained relationships cause division. Confusion about our identity and our place in the Kingdom of God has sown seeds of distrust and suspicion.

As we pray for our Bridegroom to come, it would be wise for us to consider what needs to be done to hasten His return. We have some serious growing to do. God asked us to be in service to our communities, yet too much of the church is myopic, inwardly focused. We are building our own paneled houses before taking care of the church. The world has yet to see a church ready for our Lord's return. As we gain wisdom and become *"doers of the word"* (James 1:22), we hasten the Lord's soon return. It's our move not His.

Lovingkindness Is a Lifestyle

A mature group of believers operates with lovingkindness and humility because they are comfortable with those in spiritual authority. Proper authority equips leaders and releases them into positions of service that maximize each believer's gifts and callings. In this environment, humble service is a natural result of meaningful interaction between those in authority and those who are being trained for leadership.

A Kingdom-centered call to leadership shifts the focus away from a title and toward each individual's fundamental purpose for being—to serve God and each other in the Spirit of Lovingkindness. As our gifts are recognized and nurtured, our inner human DNA takes root and blossoms. We see the difference we can make by becoming the person God calls us to be.

The next logical, pragmatic step that Yeshua shows us is to send this individual out into the field, or to borrow the analogy from this book's title, "release them back into the river." Mere human effort is not a shortcut to unity and effectiveness. An effective witness for the Kingdom is the result of a human being who embraces a higher calling by walking in harmony with God and humanity. When our hearts are engaged, our service is a beautiful blend of joyful, charismatic, and peaceful lovingkindness.

Of course we need jobs to provide income for ourselves. A good career is of inestimable value. However, unless the core of our life's purpose is dedicated to God, we won't reach the place of perfecting and maturing our being. If we choose to live for our Lord Yeshua, the service we perform will change the world He gave us. Is it too much of a stretch to consider that is why He put us here?

People who operate in roles of unselfish service gain the great sense of personal satisfaction that comes from fulfilling the divine purpose and function that God places within every human being He has created. Economic systems that fail to operate on Kingdom principles may provide jobs, goods, and services, but there are functional shortcomings that leave the participants far short of fulfilling lives, due to the fact that they lack a missional outreach that connects us to our divine calling.

Lovingkindness is not simply an attitude—it's a lifestyle.

Room to Disagree

Far too many of us, in the name of church expansion, have been building our own church, not His church—thus we are divided. As of today, the church of Yeshua the Messiah is now divided into thousands and thousands of denominations. Why? Because we are so convinced that our own method of worshipping God is better than that practiced by others, we are willing to go our own way, split His body, and to claim we still are following God. We are dangerously fragmented and easy prey for the enemy of our souls.

In response to this sad testimonial of church division, outspoken patrons of different faith communities dig their heels in deeper to justify that this is proof that his, her, or their particular sect or organization holds the ultimate solution for unity. Just that statement alone speaks of our own arrogance. The church is neither all-inclusive nor exclusive. The culture of the church is to be determined by those (note the plural) led by the Holy Spirit, whom the Lord places in authority, who understand God's word and submit to one another.

That governing body over each region or community, emulating the elder Council of Jerusalem in Acts chapter 15, makes policy decisions under the fear and admonition of the Holy Spirit. This group of mature leaders carries the voice of spiritual authority. Such a body rarely even exists in any metropolitan area in the United States. Instead we look to denominational leaders who rule from a hierarchical position that has very little understanding of the intricacies of local issues or policies faced by individual communities. Mind you, this problem is not due to lack of caring, just the logistical and geographic reality that creates the distance.

There is ample room for disagreement without disconnection about doctrines. But I'm not here to fix the church. If the church needs fixing, it will come by God's hand. Our task here is to recognize what the Lord has called us to perform and to do so. To do less is to dishonor our King and to be disobedient. To do more is to claim a spiritual authority that exceeds God's gift of grace and mercy—equally as disobedient.

In direct disobedience to the Word of God, which we claim to faithfully obey, we have broken the body of believers into competing groups, of which all too many assert superior insight and calling to fulfill the great commission that will hasten the second coming of our Lord. What we continually ignore is our own arrogance. The result is that the Lord waits for us to mature. The clear sign for us to be the one Yeshua prayed for is to be united in prayer, in fellowship, in worship, and in service. An excellent example of a united community is the *Kingdom Life Community Association* that brings dozens and dozens of multicultural pastors from differing denominations together to learn about our identity as one new man. See Noteworthy Ketches in the back of the book.

The test of our unity is our willingness to lay down our crowns and work together to serve the Lord by serving one another—to serve both alongside of believers and those yet to believe. That means, hold your breath now, with *other* churches and ministries. And this requires ongoing, daily activities. The Kingdom of Heaven is not just an event, it's a God-ordained lifestyle. Acts 2:42 details the way we are called to live in one accord.

We are a divided body, whose parts are seldom working together in unison. We are torn apart by so many winds of doctrine that any individual who looks to the church to find God has no way of knowing which part of the church truly represents Yeshua as the Head. Part of our discipling process often includes training about the superiority of our faith (obviously our own), versus the faith of others. What is touted as piety is, in fact, pride.

As we truly recognize Yeshua as the Head of the church and find our identity in Him, we will have one body and one Spirit who will be over us and through us all (see Ephesians 4:4-6 NIV). We would be united. We would move as one.

Colossians 2:19 (NIV) makes a bold statement with a broad application that we have conveniently passed by: *"They have lost connection with the head, from whom the whole body, supported and held together by its ligaments and sinews, grows as God causes it to grow."*

If the body does not work together, then we will not recognize the Head. What sure sign reveals the body does not recognize Yeshua as the Head? It's when we decide we will accept human wisdom as superseding God's wisdom. We claim to have come far, without recognizing that we are revisiting the error at Babel. Our contemporary symbols of success emphasize independence—fulfillment of selfish desires. We edify and idolize human triumphs without honoring God as the One who makes life possible, gives us our freedom, and grants us the victory.

Whenever we alter our view of the Head being Yeshua and look to human authority for our freedom, we became divided. And as the church's power and authority diminishes, the world increasingly looks elsewhere to find God. Without a shift in priorities, over time the hunger to know Him subsides. By insisting that human leadership trumps divine accountability, Western culture is usurping an authority that God alone can grant.

As we call upon our civil authorities to supply more and more of our necessities, we actually are expecting our society to provide the needs for which God designed His church to supply. Those greedy for power are happy to comply as they take the credit for helping the poor and indigent. As we relinquish control over each facet of our lives, we are being trained to look outside the believing body to civilian and social authorities in government and nongovernmental organizations for our healing, our provision, our social standing, and definition of values.

We forget humanity won't thrive without the church. In this vacuum of spiritual accountability we tend to look elsewhere than to God to fill the void we feel so acutely. As a society, we fail to recognize the position into which we are putting ourselves. By not taking the lead, we leave it to our government to determine moral moirés that only mimic righteousness. We are so fascinated with the seeming similarity to Kingdom righteousness that we unabashedly duplicate sacred ground by naming our clothes and adopting fashion statements with terminology that was once reserved for our Father in Heaven, but lack faith-based perspective on values. And the government is not only willing to do so, they feel obligated to legislate laws that restructure the divine order. This is folly. Not only won't it work, it destroys the fabric of our nation.

Because the church has failed to be unified, our posture is weak against moral and social agendas that dishonor God and humanity. As the ligaments that hold the body together get stretched and frayed, more groups emerge that pull us further and further from unity. We will not gain a united church using a divisive doctrine that ties our own hands.

We stand appalled to witness our government grow to be more unwieldy. Seeing the potential for more power, it is inevitable that the government would seek to grasp it. The vulnerability of leaders is that once they gain power, they seek to control the culture they claim to serve and cease to be subject to the will of the governed. History shows, without fail, that when leadership begins to lose sensitivity to those who are being led, that institution will fail. It's only a matter of "when," not "if." God's authority will not be mocked, swayed, or compromised.

But the damage we face goes deeper. The ironic result is that our government has switched roles. In this heavy-handed environment of social idealism the government is only accountable to itself, not its electorate. There is no ability to maintain alignment with a system of checks and balances.

When a government claims its own authority on the basis of separation of church, the state then determines moral priorities. The state takes ground that belongs exclusively to our Creator. In its own blindness, thinking that it has the primary obligation to create moral standards for its constituents, the government begins legislating and enforcing laws for issues that can only be sanctioned by the spiritual authorities that the state disempowers.

By usurping the authority that belongs solely to the Kingdom of God, such a government, thinking that it has separated itself from the church does double the damage. First, the church suffers because it no longer is the God-ordained voice for moral behavior; thus leaving the culture without a moral compass.

Second, the government, believing it has more knowledge and power than religious institutions, starts making moral choices outside of its authority, all the while claiming the right to do so because it is separate from the church. The church is God's ordained body. There is no human authority that can dictate its position. To do so is to invite judgment.

What we are missing is that the government that determines moral standards ultimately begins to operate as the church! Yes, a man-made institution, not God's authority, takes the position that they know the best way to move our society in the proper direction regarding our moral conduct.

But government cannot safely make moral decisions. It's goes against their purpose, which is to protect our boundaries, both physical and spiritual, so the church can flourish and teach the world how God wants us to love each other inside of healthy bounds. This is where freedom flourishes. The government legislates and enforces laws based upon an understanding that God's decrees are the finest, the fairest, and the ones that give the greatest degree of personal freedom.

By accepting misconstrued, humanistic social revisions for education, social agendas, and civic guidelines, we teach our society how to perform governmental functions without God.

Moreover, by accepting misconstrued, humanistic social revisions for education, social agendas, and civic guidelines, we teach our society how to perform governmental functions without God. Continuing down this path leads to further deception and the destruction of a faith-based civilization that was founded on faith in Almighty God. If we lose track of that vital principle, our future is up for grabs.

Sadly, a similar power struggle also goes on inside the church. Jeremiah speaks loud and clear to those so-called prophets who falsely claim God's authority. Too many parts of the church expound that if one doesn't adhere to their governing guidance and their particular theological doctrine for following Scripture, then you have chosen the wrong pathway to Heaven. How many churches tell their congregants they have the only way, or best way, to Heaven? The human tendency to usurp spiritual authority has seeped into Kingdom politics. In the meantime, we blindly ignore the damage to the body of believers and our world.

We are now seeing much of this in the beginning of the 21st Century. A divided church is vulnerable. In our naiveté we think we are progressing as we move further away from our Savior. We have confused vanity with virtue. King Solomon looked back over his life, having been granted more wisdom, blessings, and authority than any man alive. What did he proclaim at the end of his reign? *"Vanity of vanities, all is vanity"* (Ecclesiastes 1:2). God help us.

Alas, all is not lost. There is good news, very good news. God is near and His plans and purposes never fail. *"You visit the earth and water it, You greatly enrich it; the river of God is full of water…"* (Psalm 65:9). *"The government will be upon His shoulders,"* not ours (Isaiah 9:6). Recall Moses on the promontory, peering across the expanse of the Red Sea. God reminds him of the staff of authority that He provided: *"And Moses said to the people, 'Do not be afraid.*

Stand still, and see the salvation of the Lord, which he will accomplish for you today..." (Exodus 14:13).

God has given us His spiritual authority, the staff that Moses held, to stretch out over the waves, and to command them to separate. The Lord leaves it up to us to employ His authority and part the waters.

Diversity Not Division

At their best, denominations carry the potential to organize and support dynamic outreach. On the flip side, they also can suffocate the effectiveness of ministry by not joining cross-culturally as one in loving service. To be cross-cultural is commonly defined as connecting with other people groups. For the body of Messiah to be cross-cultural, we need to start right across the street. Our problem, and solution, is staring us in the face.

None is more obvious than our Sunday mornings. I'm sure the Lord is most pleased so many honor His Sabbath. That's a wonderful place to start. Somewhere along the line people decided that our common belief that Yeshua is the Messiah was all that was necessary for the church to be united. In so doing, we have opened the door for division.

Tens of thousands of denominations later, we still won't close the barn door and every kind of beast imaginable has claimed to belong inside the barn. Cults can use spiritual symbols to counterfeit what is sacred. They abuse the privilege our nation grants to faith-based organizations who live to honor God. This is *not* the diversity of which we speak. Paul explains:

> *For as the body is one and has many members, but all the members of that one body, being many, are one body, so also is Christ. For by one Spirit we were all baptized into one body—whether Jews or Greeks, whether slaves or free—and have all been made to drink into one Spirit. For in fact the body is not one member but many* (1 Corinthians 12:12-14).

The Word of God clarifies there is plenty of room for us to exhibit our own personalities without causing separation. God encourages us to display our unique attributes as we glorify Him. When the curtain tore revealing the Holy of Holies, it only had to tear once. We were all given equal access, through Yeshua's blood alone.

The Bible points out the need for diversity, but this separateness is pointedly identified for the purposes of our gifting, not the need for divergent denominations. Yes, some can discern spirits and others may have a word of knowledge, thus this type of gifting exemplifies different ways that the Spirit of God may be manifested among us. So God is not expecting us to be cookie cutter believers. In this arena, accepting His variety of gifts is to our advantage. It does us no good to build a community where everyone sells gas, but no one drives cars.

God does expect us to be united in our faith. While having faith that God sent His Son to save us from our sins is foundational to our belief, faith extends far beyond acceptance of Jesus as Lord and Savior. Jesus died for the forgiveness of our sins. In so doing He tore down the middle wall of separation between humanity, and specifically between Jews and Gentiles, so we can be one with God—just as Yeshua is one with God. Unity was Yeshua's last prayer to His disciples.

But God also wants us to be one with each other. The gifts and diversity within the body are designed to pull us closer together, not to become the debating points for us to justify divergent doctrines that usually tear apart what God has put together. Don't get me wrong; there's plenty of room for differing perspectives. This serves to encourage friendly debate with open dialogue. Tolerating opposing views makes us stronger and more pliable concerning theological issues. But we are not to cross the line that insists on splitting.

A good test for this condition would be to determine how often "my" church does activities with other churches. Do we worship with other churches? Do we share our facilities? By this I mean sharing the same service times and offerings. It's nice that one church allows others to use its facilities, but does this qualify as unity?

The church is big enough to have diversity in gifts and a multiplicity of perspectives on theology. On the basics we easily agree. These are repeated and well-defined in the Word. On the more obscure issues such as transubstantiation, choice of Sabbath day, tithing, fasting, etc., these are wonderful subjects for open debate. A sense of humor and a decision not to be offended can heal the wounds and close the fissure that our enemy has used to tear us apart. We must decrease that God will increase. Can't we see that our own pride is making us impotent?

During these last days our prideful superiority will be our undoing. Yeshua did not win disciples by teaching them to be better than all other fishermen. Instead, He exemplified to His followers what the prophets had been repeating to Israel for centuries:

> *He has told you, humanity, what is good, and what Adonai is seeking from you: Only to practice justice, to love mercy, and to walk humbly with your God* (Micah 6:8).

Not a hint of pride here.

Learning our Lessons

The church has not been increasing in most of the West. Of the twenty-five largest denominations, twenty-three are not growing. The church remains as God's chosen means for salvation. So when we recognize that the church is failing to expand, we need to scrutinize ourselves, not the world around us. Pinning the blame on eroding moral standards won't work. The condition of our world is the result of the ineffectiveness of the church, not the other way around. If the condition of the church is suffering from the condition of the world, then like it or not, we have no choice, other than to conclude that the church initiated, or at a minimum, allowed these problems to take root.

Because the Lord has promised us that the gates of hell will not overcome us, the church's deteriorating condition must be dealt with internally. As we have turned our discipling programs into church growth programs, we have stemmed the process for preparing our leaders to return to the River of Life.

Our focus is becoming reactive as we seek the elusive grail of church growth instead of becoming proactive to offer the cup of kindness to advance the Kingdom of God. Our exclusivity results in an unattractive church. A church that is not lively and vital belittles the very community it is called to serve, avoiding their own hand in contributing to their ills. In failing to accept our own shortcomings, we start to blame the very ones our Lord asks us to lead to faith.

Ultimately we lose trust in the church and trust in God Himself. Soon the church, not the community, becomes a target for our social ills. If the church does not actively move forward to clean up the problems that have beset its own community, then those problems swiftly come to roost within the church itself. A lukewarm response to social hardships is more dangerous than a negative one. An apathetic church becomes anemic. For an organization that owes its life to the blood of our Messiah, anemia is a death sentence.

> *An apathetic church becomes anemic. For an organization that owes its life to the blood of our Messiah, anemia is a death sentence.*

The church and its believers often undergo persecution. While this is extremely painful, it has not and will not prevent the church from expanding, even thriving. Any and every nation that persecutes the church is simply setting itself up for a nasty wakeup call. A day will come when the moral values of that nation will have so eroded that the cry for righteousness will cause the church to once again flourish in that empty space.

The issue isn't *if* such an antichurch culture will crumble, it's only a matter of time. Every society on earth that places its own well-being in front of the people of God has fallen. We would be wise to look upon this challenge. This pattern repeats itself throughout history. The question is only if we will learn these lessons before they land in our own backyard, and it's too late to recover without significant damage.

Chapter 4

Bagel Theology

A House Divided

I cannot help but think of Abraham Lincoln's great speech, based on Yeshua's words in Matthew chapter 12. Its principle can readily be applied to today's church. Simply substitute "church" for "house," then determine what has enslaved us.

> A house [church] divided against itself cannot stand. I believe this government cannot endure, permanently, half slave and half free. I do not expect the Union to be dissolved—I do not expect the house [church] to fall— but I do expect it will cease to be divided. It will become all one thing or all the other. Either the opponents of slavery will arrest the further spread of it, and place it where the public mind shall rest in the belief that it is in the course of ultimate extinction; or its advocates will push it forward, till it shall become lawful in all the States, old as well as new—North as well as South.

Abraham Lincoln was not concerned about popularity. He was concerned with truth. To speak truth, he leaned on the Holy Scriptures. These Scriptures started with the writings given by God to Moses, who led Israel out of Egyptian bondage. Slavery did not begin and end with Israel. William Wilberforce, the man who spearheaded the defeat of England's slave trade, was also a man of faith. Dr. Martin Luther King Jr. shared with us that he had "been to the mountain."

Each of these gifted leaders were shunned and despised by many. However, reappraisal through the lens of legacy has shown that their righteous acts have stood the test of time. When new movements take root in righteousness, popularity seldom results in the short term; but in the long run, God's righteousness prevails.

Our culture has adopted several "freedoms" that run contrary to the Word of God. Those spiritual leaders who oppose this direction are being ostracized by the very society that once looked to them for godly guidance. None of this can happen in a nation that glorifies God and who stand firmly on His Word. We must not reinterpret the Holy Scriptures. They are the glue that keeps our nation righteous.

As we honor God, He supplies us with manifold blessing. He has established healthy standards of morality and He promises to bless us for sustaining them. If we diminish that moral standing, then we do so at the expense of our own future.

History takes a much longer view of righteousness. There is much sorrow and bloodshed on the road to righteousness, but the Lord raises up the people of faith when the spirit of enslavement rears its ugly head. When immature leaders resort to force to control humankind's thinking, doing, or believing, God calls forth His saints.

God used Moses, Wilberforce, Lincoln, and King at history's defining crossroads to advance humanity. The benchmark of righteousness is restored as people of faith unite to overcome humanity's own inhumanity. The cost is high, but the cost of failure is the utter destruction of our freedom. That day has returned in our time.

It's time for some bagel theology. Take a bagel and slice it in half. Toast the two halves. Take one side and schmear (spread) a generous portion of cream cheese in honor of the Jews, whom God led out of Egypt to the Promised Land of "**milk** and honey." Take the second half and layer it with lox (smoked salmon) to honor the Gentiles, as Yeshua instructed His disciples to be "**fishers** of men." By now your mouth should be watering.

Each half could be eaten separately and is delicious with its own covering. However, the wonderment begins when we sandwich these two halves together. In so doing, we enter into the reunited, harmonious combination of Jew and Gentile – One in the Messiah of Israel – The One New Man. Chapter 2 of Ephesians reveals this as God's plan for "shalom." Moreover, the Hebrew word "shalom" means peace, well-being, harmony, wholeness, completeness, welfare, prosperity, and tranquility. "Shalom" is aptly applied to this restored relationship of The One New Man four times in this passage. There it is – God's perfect plan for peace! Now taste and see that the Lord is good!

And don't say it will never work. It's already being done. The community of Jewish believers in Messiah Yeshua is growing in Israel, the United States, and around the world. Every nation where there are Jews, the message of unity is on the lips of the faithful. What was once a trickle of water has become streams flowing out of the desert and through our houses of worship. This is the Lord's doing and it is marvelous in His eyes.

God designed Israel to be the foundation and cornerstone of His Kingdom. Yeshua was born, lived, and died as a Jew in Israel. To call ourselves Christians, yet reject our own Jewish roots, is to cut off our nose in spite of our face. Absurd. Playing right into the enemy's hands. To be anti-Semitic or anti-Israel is to be against our Savior. Of course Israel is not a perfect nation, but our God is the God of Israel and He has loved her unreservedly from the beginning, despite her flaws. He expects us to do the same.

The church, in an effort to fill pews, pay bills, and build bigger sanctuaries has fallen into a trap of its own making. Matthew chapters 24 and 25 lay out the consequences of rejecting Israel. History is fraught with failed empires that decided to delegitimize

Israel. The corpses from these misguided attempts to interfere with God's calling on seemingly insignificant Israel cover the bottom of the Red Sea and litter the lanes of Roman roads.

> *History is fraught with failed empires that decided to delegitimize Israel. The corpses from these misguided attempts to interfere with God's calling on seemingly insignificant Israel cover the bottom of the Red Sea and litter the lanes of Roman roads.*

How many nations will stumble over the nation with whom God made an everlasting covenant? Historically we have discovered one sure thing—the best way to end a dynasty is to attack Israel.

Chapter 5

Determining Your "Net" Worth

Nets are for catching fish. Our value as "fishers of men" is determined on the basis of what we are able to accomplish that yields more fish in our nets. This is how the Lord determines our "net" worth.

The Scriptures inform us, *"The fruit of the righteous is a tree of life, and he who wins souls is wise"* (Proverbs 11:30). This statement declares much about the purpose of a believer's life. For a man to be wise he must possess vision and purpose. He then adds to that a frame of reference that frees him to be able to apply the value system that most effectively operates within that frame of reference.

In other words, the goal of a disciple is to encourage the persons he or she encounters to follow Yeshua. In that context this proverb explains the best outcome for a life well-lived. Righteousness is a lifestyle. And a life lived righteously will yield great fruitfulness. Furthermore, that fruitfulness leads us back to the fruitfulness promised to humanity in the Garden of Eden.

We were expelled from that garden paradise due to our sin. Now Eden is attainable because of the atonement of Yeshua HaMashiach, Jesus the Messiah.

This is where we started from, and it's the place the Lord has set aside for us. The Tree of Life waits in full bloom. There is a requirement to enter—faith in Yeshua that He is the One whom God sent to seal our eternal future with Him.

And it gets better. Access is not only offered to us, we are encouraged to bring along as many others as we wish. What an awesome retirement plan!

Part II

Let's Go Fishing

Chapter 6

Casting Off

The Loading Dock

Look at all the merchandise. Stacked high as an elephant's eye. Boxes of goodies and cases of books surround you. Containers are loaded on pallets labeled with dozens of destinations. Some are nearby. Many are spread around the globe: Africa missions trip; Scenic Alaskan cruise; Baja California; Israel; Washington, DC.

The sound of an engine throttles behind you. Turning around you realize you are standing inside the cargo hold of a semi trailer stuffed to the gills. You see and hear other trucks rolling by. Your trailer is packed with everything needed to sustain you. Although roadworthy and sufficiently supplied, you aren't rolling.

Heading to the backend you pass a pile of hymnals. There's a beautiful altar and hand-finished church pews. On the way you notice a bookshelf loaded with photo albums containing pictures of smiling kids and grateful parents. Next to the tailgate hang a pair of crutches and a wheelchair. Lowering yourself to the ground, you decide to see what's delaying your departure.

The answer is obvious. There's no truck in front of your trailer. A quick glance to the side and your eyes espy a massive Peterbilt truck a few meters away. It's got all the trimmings—place to rest, fancy paintjob, airfoil, running lights, chrome stacks, etc. Back it up and we've got 18 wheels! Can't wait to get in the driver's seat.

Inviting isn't it? Your ministry has wheels. Those wheels don't do you any good if you aren't cruising. You wonder how many folks park their cars in church parking lots dreaming 'bout "Headin' down the highway." They have aspirations, but they need someone to declare, "Hitch up that trailer and take the highroad."

For a prime example, the *Rotary Club's* closely anticipated goal to eradicate polio will be one of the most significant achievements in public health since the elimination of smallpox. Please see more about this organization in the Noteworthy Ketches section in the back of the book.

How many executives with a long list of administrative skills and an MBA serve their pastors by making sure the parking lot is well-organized? Boy oh boy. Blacktop is fresh; lines are painted; exits are clear; traffic flows smoothly in and out. In the meantime, multitudes suffer because charities lack administrators and freight services. Sure your pastor needs your help, and you want to be obedient. But something is nagging you about public service that can't be satisfied by telling a parishioner where to park his Prius.

I use this illustration to encourage you to think about matching your training with missional outreach. You don't have to go far. Most churches are within a stone's throw of ministry. Just walk around the corner or down the alley. There's a rickety door that needs hinges. There's some broken glass that needs to be swept up and tossed out. There's a man, a family, without shelter. There's a strip mall in disrepair.

What would you do if Jesus were standing next to that handsome big rig (with your name painted on the driver's door) with a set of keys in His hand?

For all who want to climb in, hook up the trailer, and start being the church, I pray you are released to do just that. Be the church. Run the race set before you. Take the highway. Take it for our King! No need to look back.

And a highway will be there; it will be called the Way of Holiness; it will be for those who walk on that Way. The unclean will not journey on it; wicked fools will not go about on it. No lion will be there, nor any ravenous beast; they will not be found there. But only the redeemed will walk there, and those the Lord has rescued will return. They will enter Zion with singing; everlasting joy will crown their heads. Gladness and joy will overtake them, and sorrow and sighing will flee away (Isaiah 35:8-10).

After Baptism

Follow me and I will make you fishers of men (Matthew 4:19).

Before the foundations of the earth, Yeshua was preparing for His entry into the earth that was spoken into existence and fashioned from Heaven's throne. Across the Middle East signs of His soon-coming were everywhere. Humanity hungered for His appearance. No mere coincidence that Yeshua found His first disciples concentrating on their livelihood casting and mending nets. Yeshua caught these men just as they were getting ready to make their next catch, just as they anticipated the coming Messiah of Israel.

Upon their encounter, Yeshua bade them to follow Him. They dropped what they were doing and did so. How ironic that the Lord would employ common men with common skills, then show them how to use these skills to build the everlasting Kingdom of God.

Building the Kingdom of God does *not* require highly specialized techniques. Engineering degrees and doctorates are not prerequisites. Quite the contrary, Kingdom building uses knowledge God has already given us. Advancing Heaven's calling simply requires that we learn how to apply our God-given gifts to the process of sharing our newfound faith.

These first disciples knew how to fish. Most likely they never considered how to engage their well-developed talents in God's economy. Yeshua's request was gracious, understandable, relatable, and well within their grasp—*"Follow Me."* Had they not sensed that this was the One for whom they were waiting, it's doubtful they would have budged. But this Man approached in a kind and humble manner, asking if they wanted to keep doing what they had been doing within a new context. No problem. Off they went.

Notable that Yeshua did what He was asking others to do. He was capable of superhuman results, but did not require that of others. Now we know that the results He achieved were beyond measure. That was His way of showing us what was available if we would just follow Him. To model this behavior, Yeshua decided to be baptized in the Jordan River. In that culture, a dipping or ritual purification bath, known as a *mikvah*, was not an unusual experience.

When a person comes to faith there are a few steps of obedience that assure the new believer gets off on the right foot in his or her walk of faith. First comes an expression of faith, with the acknowledgment that we need God for salvation. This commitment includes the confession of our sin, which leads us to repentance, a turning away from our old way of living. Yeshua is the only person who ever walked the planet who did not need to repent.

Next comes immersion into the waters of baptism, representing death, burial, and rising up again in resurrection life. This is a statement of faith for both ourselves and for the faith-based community of our commitment to follow Jesus as our Lord and Savior.

As a person lifts up out of these waters a first breath is taken. A fresh infilling of air accompanies a release from Heaven. A divine download of Kingdom purpose by means of the *Ruach HaKodesh* (The Holy Spirit) regenerates our souls and begins to guide us on a journey that will unfold daily for the rest of our lives.

When John the Baptist (Yochanan the Immerser) baptized Jesus (Yeshua) the heavens opened and the Ruach HaKodesh (The Holy Spirit) descended upon Him like a dove. This is the picture of what

God did for His Son, just as He does for us, by His Spirit. Rising above the waves, we follow Yeshua's example.

From this point forward our training begins. Most refer to this process as "discipling." Usually there are classes for new believers. There are Scripture verses to study. We are introduced to the Bible in a new light as the uncompromising Word of God. We start learning how to navigate through God's blueprint to build His Kingdom.

During this honeymoon with the Lord, new revelation is common. We are rediscovering the meaning and purpose for our lives. This is also the season where each faith community determines to imprint their interpretation of God's Word and His destiny upon new believers in terms of their particular perspective on how we are to walk with God.

We have lifted the new believer out of the waters of baptism, dried them off, and informed them of their new identity. Unfortunately, this next step of "discipling" often takes the form of branding. We want the newborn to take on the name of our group, our denomination, our church, our congregation, if you will, our club.

> *Our church leaders have inadvertently started to make the church exclusive instead of inclusive.*

The focus of training becomes more institutionalized. We are being clothed in the garments of Yeshua, but the tailoring swiftly takes on human dimensions. We are definitely excited by our new birth and identity, yet separated from the environment from whence we came. The message is clear. We are informed that we must be schooled before we can go back into the world. Our church leaders have inadvertently started to make the church exclusive instead of inclusive.

We are learning what it means to be "in the world," but not "of the world." Our new life comes with a new perspective on living. But during this transitional phase there is a potential danger that lurks here. There is a high price to this disconnection from the world and reconnection into the Kingdom of God that has been overlooked and it is costing the community of believers dearly.

By delaying the release of new believers back into the swollen streams of humanity, we lose the fresh enthusiasm and infilling of the Holy Spirit that makes witnessing our faith an exhilarating, revitalizing, joyful experience. When we separate the new believer from his or her environment to disciple them, we unwittingly begin to snuff out the fresh fire of the Holy Spirit.

Just when the light burns the brightest, just when new hope has been kindled, just when we are ready to ignite the world with the Good News of Yeshua—we pull our nets of freshly filled believers away from the river of life and set them into a dry, intellectual environment for the purpose of training in the intricacies of "our" faith.

Of course we must train new believers. This is good and necessary. The issue at hand concerns how this training should be accomplished. There was good reason for Yeshua to call upon fishermen to build His Kingdom. These men were unschooled, not professional students. There is a high likelihood that most of the first disciples would not have known how to read.

Please remember, Yeshua asked us to follow Him, not our fellow humanity. When we start discipling new believers to look like ourselves, instead of looking like our Lord, we commandeer something pure and simple and try to make it our own. The Kingdom of God has suffered from our own arrogance. The fallout from this error has manifold implications.

Yeshua laid out clear instructions that we may receive once we recognize the foolishness of trying to reconfigure His ways. Just as Peter needed to be rescued from sinking and placed back in the boat, Yeshua will reinstall our faith and revitalize His church. His Word still stands: *"Follow Me."*

Chapter 7

Catching Fish

The self-proclaimed objective of Yeshua's ministry is to reach us and teach us how to be *fishers of men* (Matthew 4:19; Mark 1:17). Fishing defines the initial point of contact for Yeshua's outreach to His disciples as He first locates them casting and repairing their nets. Correspondingly, Peter and his cohorts are again fishing at the conclusion of his earthly ministry. Imagine the joy as Peter the "big fisherman" realizes it is indeed the resurrected Lord who calls from the shore of the Sea of Galilee, *"Cast the net on the right side of the boat, and you will find some"* (John 21:6). No wonder he jumped into the water as he hastened to rejoin his Master.

Yeshua meant business when He told those fishermen they would be fishers of men. Today we know our Lord's instruction, *"Follow Me,"* was His introduction to a new covenant between God and humanity. The sublime result of obeying this divine ordinance is nothing less than eternal salvation. Employing this simple illustration of fishing, Yeshua both caught and taught His disciples. The premise presented and practiced two thousand years ago remains unchanged—God is calling us to be His children as He teaches us His ways.

Just how are we supposed to fish? Is there a difference between how the church currently evangelizes the world and what Yeshua instructed? Sadly, the answer is yes. Yeshua taught timeless principles. Failing to follow these same guidelines, surely the church will suffer. This is the dilemma we face today.

I would suggest that both our catching and releasing need scrutiny. Most of our teaching focuses on catching. We relish the biblical stories of individuals and multitudes coming to faith. The Word of God tells us that it is the Holy Spirit who leads us to faith. So how do we open ourselves to this move of the Holy Spirit? Let's allow the Holy Scriptures to speak from the Gospel of Luke 5:1-11:

> *So it was, as the multitude pressed about Him* [Yeshua] *to hear the word of God, that He stood by the Lake of Gennesaret, and saw two boats standing by the lake; but the fishermen had gone from them and were washing their nets. Then He got into one of the boats, which was Simon's, and asked him to put out a little from the land. And He sat down and taught the multitudes from the boat.*
>
> *When He had stopped speaking, He said to Simon, "Launch out into the deep and let down your nets for a **catch**."*
>
> *But Simon answered and said to Him, "Master, we have toiled all night and **caught** nothing; nevertheless at Your word I will let down the net." And when they had done this, they **caught** a great number of fish, and their net was breaking. So they signaled to their partners in the other boat to come and help them. And they came and filled both the boats, so that they began to sink. When Simon Peter saw it, he fell down at Jesus' knees, saying, "Depart from me, for I am a sinful man, O Lord!"*
>
> *For he and all who were with him were astonished at the **catch** of fish which they had taken; and so also were James and John, the sons of Zebedee, who were partners with Simon. And Jesus said to Simon, "Do not be afraid. From now on you will **catch** men." So when they had brought their boats to land, they forsook all and followed Him.*

These fishermen were shown that their efforts were futile without God's help. Likewise, by following Yeshua's instructions, the catch was so overwhelming that they needed other fishermen just to handle the haul. When Yeshua starts His church, the response is so remarkable that Peter collapses at Yeshua's feet and confesses his sin and unworthiness. His seasoned shipmates are *"astonished."*

Yeshua shows mastery over a domain that the fishermen previously viewed as their privileged estate. Even the nets can't contain the catch and their boats begin to sink under the load. Assuredly, this is divine intervention. This is a game-changer. That's what fishing with Yeshua looks like!

It is at this moment of revelation, as all these fishermen realized they have encountered a miraculous move of God, Yeshua reassures Peter, *"Don't be afraid."* Our initial response to the supernatural is often fear. When we encounter something that defies our ability to comprehend, it can be perplexing and paralyzing.

Most divine encounters in the Bible start with the necessity of a heavenly host informing the observer, *"Don't be afraid."* Just as the very moment of salvation is deeply imprinted in the mind of most believers, this is nothing less than discovering the meaning of life. When the answer appears in the form of a Hebrew Prophet staring us in the face, our lives change course and there's no turning back.

The beauty of this overwhelming catch is magnified when the fishermen call for their partners in the other boat to come alongside to help with the haul. The church, flat out, is not ready for the coming revival. We will be calling upon every part of the body to come together to assist in gathering the huge harvest of souls who will pour into the Kingdom of Heaven.

The ingathering will be so great that no single church or denomination; no alliance or affiliation of faith; no organization or corporation will be able to handle the vast numbers of fish who will swim into the Lord's nets. Unity in the church will not be established through well-thought theology. Unity will come as a necessity.

There will be persecution against the church. The world will be forced to make a choice. The church has not appeared on the outside to be a popular place. A great deal of finger pointing has occurred during recent years. The church has been profiled as rigid, dated, out of touch, protective of pedophiles, insensitive to gays, unwilling to sympathize with the unwed, and unable to match the pace of modern society. In short, our peers are viewing us as incompetent.

Nevertheless, as these appointed times unfold, there will be a power and presence of God to touch the hearts of humanity, the likes of which we have never seen. The church is entering the era of empty nets, initiating the Great Awakening. This season precedes the Second Coming, but first, these times must unfold.

The world brazenly disqualifies the Kingdom of God as it cries out for supernatural help. We are called to assist those who resist. Is this why we've been told the harvest is plentiful, but the workers are few? (Matthew 9:37) Being a member of a church will not be for the faint of heart in the coming days.

Ministry is messy. Drowning victims require caution, but they seek salvation. Loving our neighbor can be a tough call. We didn't expect the catch to be so vast. We haven't prepared ourselves for the coming outpouring. How are we going to clean so many fish?

> *Our world sorely needs us, yet we seek the great escape...*

In the meantime, we dreamily gaze upon distant shores, praying the Lord will call us to breakfast on the beach. We pray that He will not tarry; hoping we won't be left behind. Our world sorely needs us, yet we seek the great escape, instead of dropping our nets on the other side of the boat.

Cleaning Fish

When the church goes fishing for souls, it usually does so with the purpose of expanding its population within the confines of its own denomination.

When most churches adopt a new convert to faith, there is a pathway laid out for discipling. There may be membership classes; perhaps joining a home group; Bible study is a must; often a mentor is assigned. Without any derogatory intent, I would refer to this initiation into church culture as "cleaning the fish."

While we may not figuratively gut or filet our "freshly caught" believer, there are certain similarities when it comes to cleaning fish. There are parts of that fish that no longer will be needed in the Kingdom of God. Old habits, lifestyle choices, language, and behaviors are now seen in a new light. Our great hope is that the conversion experience initiates these changes. Most folks look at discipling as a lengthy, strenuous, labor-intensive process designed to adjust a person's character so they will learn how to walk and talk "like one of us."

Discipling begins by sending young hatchlings back to school. However these small fry are now swimming in a different classroom. In the Western world, this season of rebuilding happens inside the confines of a church. We are intent on giving the best scriptural foundation for our faith that we can communicate. Although this path is well-traveled, this is where our methodology takes a different avenue than our Messiah's. Let's not lose track that our goal is to be released back into the river; not kept in the pond.

Learning to study and divide the Word of God is an absolute necessity to grow in the Lord. None would argue this requirement. The question posed here concerns our methodology for training. It is at this point where a denominational identity can overstep the teaching arena with a predetermined process that presumes we should be grooming small fry to take on the appearance of fish of our own choosing.

Yeshua did not operate in this fashion. Yeshua was hands-on. He traveled alongside the lost sheep. He shared the journey. He sat by fires. He walked down roads. He showed up. And as soon as His saints had tasted the Kingdom of Heaven, He sent them out. Our surrounding environment is the ideal stream to get wet and learn how to swim with new strokes and breathing techniques.

It was in the world that the followers of Yeshua would learn how to minister, grow, and proliferate. Immersion into outreach cleans fish as we interact with our surrounding life streams. Yeshua said, "Go!"

"Go!" One word. Two letters.

Transformed Lives

The best example of a healthy church is transformed lives. And the best way to transform a life is through missional outreach. The world is the place Yeshua chose to clean His fish. His *talmidim*, or disciples, were cleansed on the highways and byways of Israel. They entered homes and marketplaces. They were present with the people.

The service-minded church enriches the community where it has been planted. A disciple is transformed as he and she transforms the community. What better way to instruct new believers than to send them into an environment where lovingkindness provides the foundation? This is what Yeshua did. He sent His disciples out!

Jesus identified Himself as *"the one whom God sent."* In turn, we are to be identified as "the ones sent by God." Our character and our calling exemplify Yeshua. We learn about the Father by imitating His Son. Thus others will learn how to see His Son, by viewing His disciples. We are salt and light. We must be tasted and we must be seen. It's right there in Psalm 34:8, God wants us to experience Him!

> *Oh, taste and see that the Lord is good; blessed is the man who trusts in Him!*

Yeshua knew that direct contact between believers and the rest of the world is the quickest, most effective way to demonstrate the Kingdom of God is at hand. (The terms "Kingdom of God" and "Kingdom of Heaven" are used interchangeably here as they are in the Bible.)

When Yeshua stated that this Kingdom was "at hand," He illustrated it was near, within reach, close enough to touch and feel. The Kingdom of God is to be experienced, not just talked about. How is the world going to know the gospel is for real if the church only displays its identity in the meeting hall of their local chapter rather than on the streets of our communities where hurting people need help?

And what does the Lord tell us about recognizing His disciples? That's right, it's by our love. Our commandment from Yeshua is to follow two bedrock principles: First, our love for God; second, our love for one another. It makes absolutely no sense to keep that love hidden from the world Yeshua is teaching us to reach.

> *By this all will know that you are My disciples, if you have love for one another* (John 13:35).

So if the fundamental identifying feature of a disciple is our love for one another, that behooves the church to instruct disciples out in the open. We are not asking the church to do anything new. We are following Yeshua and His ways.

Chapter 8

Discipling Is a Contact Sport

Cutting the Cost

Due to a limited vision of missions, one of the first corners we cut is the cost of discipling. Have we forgotten that this is the future of the church? We've heard the excuses: 1) Discipling requires lots of experience; 2) It's time consuming; 3) You need to have a deep understanding of theology; 4) There's no budget, etc.

The real question is, "Just how did Yeshua teach His disciples? Now that we know the answer, that's what we should be doing. Too many conclude that unless we have a university degree and a few initials after our names, we aren't qualified to be teachers and mentors. This presumes discipling is complicated and best suited for deacons and elders. Not so.

Isn't this why we love to see fishermen leading the charge? Yeshua and His followers confounded the Sanhedrin—the religious authorities of their day. How could such common, unschooled people teach the public and baffle the most qualified, well-disciplined theologians? The answer is inescapable—the Holy Spirit had touched these men. The wisdom of God had manifested in the lives of the least qualified theologians in Israel. God loves to confound the wise with the simple.

We are reminded of Yeshua's inquiry about His identity:

> *"But what about you?"* [Yeshua] *asked. "Who do you say I am?" Simon Peter answered, "You are the Messiah, the Son of the living God." Jesus replied, "Blessed are you, Simon son of Jonah, for this was not revealed to you by flesh and blood, but by my Father in heaven"* (Matthew 16:15-17 NIV).

Yeshua is telling us that only God can reveal such knowledge. Our own hearts long to hear such affirmation from the Lord. Our wisdom is not measured by what we have learned from human instruction. As edifying as this may be, it quickly fades as compared to the godly wisdom given to us from Heaven's realm.

> ## *Our world hungers for real truth because it no longer knows where to find it. But we do.*

The indwelling of the Holy Spirit is the best testimony of our relationship with our Maker. Discovering this alongside other believers is inspiring. Besides, witnessing the testimony of a new disciple as he or she encounters unbelievers is an irresistible statement of a life transformed. This captures the attention of a world that has redefined truth into a relative, even flexible, concept. When a new believer speaks truth, every head in the room turns. The community knows this person. Our world hungers for real truth because it no longer knows where to find it. But we do.

Our investment in discipling is an investment into nurturing our newborn. The return on this investment is priceless, plus the church grows exponentially. When people come to faith their flames burn brightly. You can feel the heat. You can see the light. Of course we don't want to hide that brilliance under a basket.

> *Whoever believes in me, as the Scripture has said, rivers of living water will flow from within them* (John 7:38 NIV).

Discipling is a contact sport. Sending new believers out to impact our community starts the release of *dunamis* or dynamic power. We can study the Holy Scriptures all day and night, but if we neglect the lives within a few steps of our houses of worship, our gospel fails to be pertinent.

Missional outreach is the seedbed for discipling. New believers, just as newborn infants, are our hope for the future. If we avoid putting these "fresh fish" back into the flow of life, the world misses viewing a brightly burning vessel filled with the Holy Spirit, manifesting God's love.

Recall the face of Moses radiating the glory of God after his encounters in the wilderness. Everyone who observed the prophet knew he had been in intimate contact with God Almighty. It's no different for us than it was for Moses. God wants to be near to His children, and most of all, He wants us to know that He loves us. The glory on each face is an inevitable outcome of experiencing His presence.

A healthy discipling program costs practically nothing. Yeshua's model entails hands-on instruction from the Word, enhanced by face-to-face encounters "out in the field." To do one without the other is to only receive half the loaf of the Bread sent down by Heaven. Half a loaf is better than none. But we will be short-changed for what the Lord has in store for those who follow Him. Recall the divided bagel is greatly enhanced when Jew and Gentile are reassembled with all the trimmings God has prepared for us in His glorious galley. Mouthwatering.

God gives us both halves. There is a great reward for assisting others. Yes, it takes some effort. Studying the Word confirms our belief that it is divinely inspired. This is the groundwork necessary to strengthen our faith. Fishing for men requires learning God's will (preparing our nets), then executing His desires (go fishing).

Far more beneficial than economic investing is personal investing. Caring for the sick, helping the elderly, and reconstructing broken lives is the most rewarding experience a human being can have—bar none. Personal connection is the goal that directs professional conduct. In turn we receive the highest yield on investment. Our world glorifies status and position. Our Lord glorifies humble mercy. That's the fruit that lasts.

To meaningfully touch people, the gloves have to come off.

> *To meaningfully touch people, the gloves have to come off.*

And how does the world respond to the touch of our Lord? The woman at the well immediately went into her town to share the good news. The men on the way to Emmaus returned to Jerusalem to testify of Yeshua's resurrection. They couldn't wait to share their stories. The light of our Messiah can never be quenched.

An astonished public witnessed Yeshua's unreserved immersion into the living streams of the poor in spirit. Instead of avoiding the unclean, the Lord sought them out. He wasn't concerned about the opinions of religious authorities. He was about His Father's business. Yeshua was, is, and will always be, the Living Water.

What did John the Baptist inquire of Yeshua from his jail cell?

> *And John, calling two of his disciples to him, sent them to Jesus, saying, "Are You the Coming One, or do we look for another?" When the men had come to Him, they said, "John the Baptist has sent us to You, saying, 'Are You the Coming One, or do we look for another?'" And that very hour He cured many of infirmities, afflictions, and evil spirits; and to many blind He gave sight. Jesus answered and said to them, "Go and tell John the things you have seen and heard: that the blind see, the lame walk, the lepers are cleansed, the deaf hear, the dead are raised, the poor have the gospel preached to them. And blessed is he who is not offended because of Me"* (Luke 7:19-23).

With all deference to many of the wisest theologians and teachers in the best seminaries on the planet, Yeshua's response does not hinder classroom activities; it enhances our walk of faith.

The fishermen from the Sea of Tiberius walked with Him. They witnessed the Lord's miracles. Yeshua's classroom is the world, thereby giving us living examples to apply to the Holy Scriptures.

That's what inspired our patriarchs to inscribe the Gospel accounts testifying to the truth that the Kingdom of God was at hand. The best witness of believers goes beyond what is happening in their own lives; the confirming testimony comes when one believer teaches another to fish. That's the place disciples of our King learn the art of fishing for men—back in the water.

Advancing the Kingdom of God commences with witnessing. Genuine witnessing that exemplifies a sincere heart of compassion opens the fishnets of salvation. That newly saved soul is just dying to share his or her faith. Evangelism begins when we obey our Lord's beckoning.

God's favor shows up the moment we start instructing His followers. Effective discipling strikes at the very heart of the gospel. As Yeshua draws a new believer into His nets, the process of instruction naturally draws us to make contact with the needy. Outreach takes us back upstream to the spawning beds where life ends and life begins.

Sending Out the Saints

Once Yeshua demonstrated His ministry of lovingkindness, verified through signs and wonders, His *talmidim* were hungry to step out and flex their own spiritual muscles. Knowing a believer must rely on the Holy Spirit, in a true test of faith, Yeshua releases His fishermen to fish for humanity without visible means of support. He starts with His twelve most trusted:

> *Then He called His twelve disciples together and gave them power and authority over all demons, and to cure diseases. He sent them to preach the kingdom of God and to heal the sick. And He said to them, "Take nothing for the journey, neither staffs nor bag nor bread nor money; and do not have two tunics apiece."* (Luke 9:1-3).

Next came the release of the Seventy:

> *After these things the Lord appointed seventy others also, and sent them two by two before His face into every city and place where He Himself was about to go. Then He said to them, "The harvest truly is great, but the laborers are few; therefore pray the Lord of the harvest to send out laborers into His harvest. Go your way; behold, I send you out as lambs among wolves. Carry neither moneybag, knapsack, nor sandals; and greet no one along the road"* (Luke 10:1-4).

Those sent went without any tangible means of protection, guidance, or sustenance. Without a cloak, they lacked the covering of a congregation or denomination. Without shoes, this was a sure sign of poverty. Without food, money, change of clothes, etc. We get the picture. This was a true test of faith. These men relied completely on the Holy Spirit for protection, guidance, and sustenance.

What do we learn from this? The best way to transform our world is to transform our disciples by returning them to the waters where they learned to swim. Here the fish can properly reproduce. Here young fry can frolic in the Spirit. Other fish will taste and see the Kingdom of Heaven. Discipling is not an exclusive private event behind closed doors. Disciples need to see the world through their new eyes, and the world needs to see the changed character of new believers.

This is how we raise healthy fish. These fish have been cleaned and weaned. They don't exist on spiritual milk; they know how to survive in the river. Then, as they head out into the deep waters, they are secure in their new identity.

> *And how can anyone preach unless they are sent?*
> (Romans 10:15 NIV)

A Honeymoon with Him

The best biblical homiletics (interpretation of words) is gained by learning vocabulary in light of both historical and proximal (immediate surroundings) contexts. Just as we investigate the rocky shoals where we cast our nets, we need to inspect the character of our culture.

We study the history of Israel to grasp the context of the Holy Scriptures. We see how Yeshua responded to His environment. He modeled this behavior so we too would know how to respond to our own contemporary culture. When the church distances itself from the society that it needs to reach, we send the wrong signal to those who need us the most.

Yeshua mandates that we release those who have come to faith back into the river from which they were drawn. These new babes in the Lord may look like their former persona, but they don't swim like them. These "clean" fish exhibit confidence and composure. Big fish that only puff themselves up no longer intimidate them.

Life for a new believer is never boring. Everything is new again. Recall those heady days when you first fell in love. Nothing could hurt you. You were immune to criticism. It doesn't matter *what* you know. All that matters is *who* you know. And now you know Yeshua, the Messiah of Israel. This love story never grows old.

This is the honeymoon offered by Heaven. Those early days of walking with the Lord are ever so precious. Nothing compares with someone falling in love. We want to experience this joy. We revel in sharing this with others, just as we treasure being close to anyone who is discovering pure love.

Renowned evangelist John Wesley understood this principle. His following quotations attest to his enthusiasm for reaching his world, "Beware you be not swallowed up in books! An ounce of love is worth a pound of knowledge."

Wesley made sure his audience witnessed the Holy Spirit at work. Just preaching wasn't enough. To share the gospel for him was to dig deep into one's soul and draw every ounce of your being into your message: "Catch on fire and others will love to come watch you burn."

Here was a man who would not hide his passion under a basket. He knew the brighter you shine, the easier it is to witness the love of God. He wanted his listeners to encounter the glory Moses experienced when the prophet met God.

Chapter 9

How to Fish

Fish or Cut Bait

Fishing is not a passive activity. Whether netting schools of submerged sardines from the decks of a sailing trawler or sitting peacefully aboard a drifting dory, the art of fishing tests our talents. The very virtue of patience finds its home in the heart of a fisherman.

Lest we be confused, patience is not a synonym for passivity. Effective fishing requires us to be ever ready to land a big one. While viewing the motionless line disappearing into the depths, a fisherman must be prepared to swiftly set the hook as the fish takes the bait. His mind may be mulling the mysteries of the universe, but he's focused on the filament that connects him to his conquest. A good fisherman is calm, quiet, collected; yet poised to spring into action.

Just as we gather but glimpses of the spiritual world, we have to keep our eyes on the bobber or the tip of the fishing pole to alert us to activity in the hidden realm. Notably, first signs are subtle, so keen concentration can decipher the difference between a feast of freshly fried rainbow from the river versus cracking a can of tuna that has been gathering dust in the kitchen cabinet.

So if a person learns how to fish in the natural, applying these talents to the supernatural is less of a stretch. When a fisherman is not casting a line, he's thinking about the best way to catch a fish the next time he heads to the waters. Specifically, this means strategizing which bait is ideal.

This principle is no different inside the Kingdom of Heaven. When our thoughts become earnest prayers, the Lord sets events into motion. As the disciples discovered, even the best-laid plans of the most accomplished fishermen will not gain satisfactory results unless the Spirit of God moves the fish into the right position.

Preparing the proper bait in the finest fashion yields the best outcome. The wrong bait, or even the right bait mistakenly displayed, fails to attract our finned friends beneath the foam. We are entering a hidden domain that will require the mutual cooperation of both gifted fishermen and the expression of godly gifts. Yeshua chose those who were ready to learn and to submit to Him. He'll choose us too; just as soon as we desire.

"Are you going to fish or cut bait?"

Let's revisit the colloquialism, "Are you going to fish or cut bait?" This question is commonly directed to elicit a reactive response. Such a derogatory expression usually implies the listener is lazy or lethargic. But to a serious fisherman, preparing the bait is an essential part of a winning game plan.

The question being asked is really, "Are you going to go fishing, or are you thinking about how you are going to catch a fish?" The assumption is that just thinking about catching a fish doesn't land a perch in the ketch (sailboat). But let's hold right here. What was Yeshua telling us as He declared, "Follow me and I will make you fishers of men?"

Yeshua wasn't just instructing the fishermen how to cast a net. No. He reeducates them as to how to approach every aspect of fishing. He casts a new light on life. Because the desired result was changing—catching men—the game plan needed to change as well.

The Lord showed His disciples a much grander goal can be achieved by following His principles for fishing and applying them to the salvation of human souls. For the men who sailed the Sea of Galilee and whose hearts hungered for the coming Messiah, such an invitation was imperative.

Yeshua finds them as they prepare their nets, getting ready for the next day's work. What a perfect picture of planning for provision. For these eager hands, fishing was their job, their livelihood. It was a commercial enterprise, which required a group effort.

The night before this encounter, Yeshua had prayed to God. Those who were to be chosen were selected by divine providence. They were primed. With God, *"To everything there is a season, a time for every purpose under heaven"* (Ecclesiastes 3:1).

These willing souls wanted to be close to God and they knew how to fish. Or more appropriately stated, they thought they knew how to fish. When the Lord directed the disciples to the deep, He most certainly knew the fish would take the bait, or if you will, be caught in their nets.

For our purposes here, let's take a quick glance at the essential elements for weekend getaways to the lakes and streams in order to illuminate some fundamental principles. A seasoned fisherman knows that fishing without proper bait is futile. If we don't secure the right fly or select the best-suited salmon egg, the silvery swimmers will ignore our efforts. Fish may not be extremely intelligent, but they aren't dumb. They have their scruples. In fact, they can be downright finicky, frustrating even the most experienced frontiersman.

So let's reconsider cutting bait. A wise fisherman uses his time away from the watercourse contemplatively. When we aren't casting our line, we are pondering how our illusive prey is eyeing the slipstream of the rapids.

Our quarry is hungry and he hunts for something savory to swallow. Our task is to supply that need by understanding his environment— season, time of day, weather, flies, insects, larvae, eggs, etc.—that give us the insight to predict his response to our bait.

Many is the time an angler has espied the monster of the fishing hole; who casts his line to just the right spot, but the savvy survivor won't go for the barbed prize. Just what does this bully of the backwash want for breakfast? Fishing requires forensic foresight, as well as a touch of luck.

Fishing is a singularly satisfying blend of art and science. A resolute sportsperson knows the need for tools. The right rod and reel. A good hat, vest, and waders. Sunscreen and dark glasses. All these increments make fishing more enjoyable and productive, but without bait we are asking the fish to bite on a raw metal hook. It just ain't gonna happen.

Using the right bait transfigures the outing to the backwoods waterway from a long frustrating sweaty day warding off swarms of mosquitoes, into an action-packed thriller. Fables abound recalling great adventures entailing invigorating exercise, scaling perilous cliffs, dousing in frigid waters, fashioning flies, fiercely fighting fish, overflowing baskets of brookies, and fending off jealous bears.

For all the time and energy invested into an act that appears to be simplistic, fishing, especially the way Yeshua guides, is the most productive pursuit a human being can enjoy. Lest we forget, it is loaves and fishes that the Master multiplies to feed the multitudes. Fishing is the forerunner for miracles.

Thus, a person who learns how to "cut bait" by employing the appropriate tools, developing a proper understanding of the fish and its surroundings, and learning the self-disciple to be ready when the big one strikes, will become an effective fisherman for the Kingdom of God.

Fishing in Kingdom of Heaven parlance is known as evangelization. In the United States, this essential missional outreach seldom takes place among the great majority of believers. What has happened? Thinking about fishing or cutting bait is not enough.

People of action both cut their bait and go fishing!

It will be people of action who both cut their bait *and* go fishing. Hopefully you have been blessed with an employer who understands and appreciates the Great Commission and our Lord's call that we "Go fishing!" Now just where did I put my tackle box…

> *And from the days of John the Baptist until now the kingdom of heaven suffers violence, and the violent take it by force* (Matthew 11:12).

Fishing from the Pier

Recreational fishing is fun. It's a great way to enjoy the outdoors and get some fresh air. Tossing a line in the water is most relaxing. We can settle back and take the time to contemplate the issues of life. Fishing is a way of searching for deeper values. We ponder the depth of our souls as we probe the waters below.

For the joy of fishing itself, a fishing pole off the edge of a pier is a marvelous pastime. While we may be able to reel in enough fish to feed a few people, commercial fishermen head out to the deep for a big catch. This requires a different approach. On the open seas, when we are looking for a big haul, we use nets.

Fish like to school. They enjoy the company of others. They often travel in groups of similar species. When Yeshua beckons, these fish willingly swim straight into the nets. Why did Yeshua exhibit this to us?

There is the obvious parable instructing the fishermen to cast their nets on the other side of the boat, despite a full night's frustration at catching nothing. But I'd like to look at how Yeshua catches one fish as the model for how to catch many.

Nicodemus was a member of the Sanhedrin, the elite leadership of Israel. The term Sanhedrin literally means "sitting together." As an elder statesman, Nicodemus risked his reputation by visiting Yeshua. Under the cover of darkness he sought out the One who was in the epicenter of all the controversy with Nicodemus' fellow leaders. He wanted answers and he wasn't getting them inside the government. He knew God was at work, but he couldn't figure out how. He wanted the truth. John's words in chapter 3 expose nothing less than his sovereign design for world history.

Yeshua wastes no words. He tells Nicodemus, "*You must be born again.*" In what is the most poignant and persistently quoted passage of the Holy Scriptures, the stage is set for us all to see God's plan for humanity. Yeshua tells Nicodemus that a person must be submitted to God to know who God really is. Nicodemus asks, "How can these things be?"

> *There was a man of the Pharisees named Nicodemus, a ruler of the Jews. This man came to Jesus by night and said to Him, "Rabbi, we know that You are a teacher come from God; for no one can do these signs that You do unless God is with him."*
>
> *Jesus answered and said to him, "Most assuredly, I say to you,* **unless one is born again, he cannot see the kingdom of God***."*
>
> *Nicodemus said to Him, "How can a man be born when he is old? Can he enter a second time into his mother's womb and be born?"*
>
> *Jesus answered, "Most assuredly, I say to you, unless one is born of water and the Spirit, he cannot enter the kingdom of God. That which is born of the flesh is flesh, and that which is born of the Spirit is spirit. Do not marvel that I said to you, 'You must be born again.'*
>
> ***The wind blows where it wishes,*** *and you hear the sound of it, but cannot tell where it comes from and where it goes. So is everyone who is born of the Spirit."*
>
> *Nicodemus answered and said to Him, "How can these things be?"*
>
> *Jesus answered and said to him, "Are you the teacher of Israel, and do not know these things? Most assuredly, I say to you, We speak what We know and testify what We have*

*seen, and you do not receive Our witness. If I have told you earthly things and you do not believe, how will you believe if I tell you heavenly things? No one has ascended to heaven but **He who came down from heaven, that is, the Son of Man** who is in heaven. **And as Moses lifted up the serpent in the wilderness, even so must the Son of Man be lifted up, that whoever believes in Him should not perish but have eternal life.** For God so loved the world that **He gave His only begotten Son, that whoever believes in Him should not perish but have everlasting life.** For God did not send His Son into the world to condemn the world, but that **the world through Him might be saved*** (John 3:1-17).

In this oft-quoted passage, Yeshua uses Torah to answer each of Nicodemus' questions. Declaring, *"He who came down from heaven... is the Son of Man,"* Yeshua takes Nicodemus back through Israel's history, territory with which a *"teacher of Israel"* would be intimately familiar.

Just as with His first disciples, Yeshua uses a context familiar to Nicodemus. Yeshua shows him that if he wants to delve into the answers to his queries, he is going to need to go deep. The leader is asking, *"How can these things be?"* Yeshua reveals the magnitude of His ministry to the leader. To go fishing with Yeshua is to be reminded of Israel's story as it is recorded for all to see God's plan for salvation.

First Yeshua reminds Nicodemus of Israel's time in the wilderness following the miraculous crossing of the Red Sea. I refer you to Numbers 21:4-9. Here we find a supernatural event as God demonstrates His sovereignty when desert vipers attack the children of Israel.

It is no accident that a snake, just as the one from the Garden of Eden who enticed Adam and Eve to sin, would be lifted up above the heads of the Israelites to gaze upon. By looking upon that bronze serpent their lives were saved from the deadly bite of vipers.

Can we possibly overlook the indelible image of the Son of God also being raised up on a cross to grant us salvation by forgiving us our sins? None other than the divine hand of God has orchestrated this. Yeshua took on sin and was made a spectacle to save us.

In one of Torah's most dramatic Messianic prophecies we observe Israel disregard Moses' standing with God by voicing their complaints. This results in God releasing venomous snakes who bit the people. Many Israelites died. Realizing their grievous error, the people approach Moses, *"We sinned when we spoke against the Lord and against you. Pray that the Lord will take the snakes away from us."*

This historic event would most certainly be a well-known topic of study and discussions among the Sadducees and Pharisees, the foremost groups comprising the Sanhedrin. A lethal problem was averted when the Lord instructed Moses to make a snake out of bronze (a clear violation of forming a graven image, reminiscent of the serpent who tempted Adam and Eve) and place it on a pole that was raised for the viewing of all who had sinned. *"So Moses made a bronze snake and put it up on a pole. Then when anyone was bitten by a snake and looked at the bronze snake, they lived"* (Numbers 21:9 NIV).

Little could Nicodemus grasp that such a confrontation of evil in the wilderness would foreshadow the Lord's dealing with the sins of humanity; or that his inquiry would be used by God to confirm Messiah's identity. Nicodemus was being shown the ultimate purpose for Yeshua—to be raised high on the cross, as He took all our sins upon Himself.

In turn, once Israel views the symbol of their own sin, raised high upon the pole for all to see and repents by asking God for forgiveness, He would restore their lives! What a dramatic preview of Yeshua's crucifixion! Yeshua instructs the teacher, *"And as Moses lifted up the serpent in the wilderness, even so must the Son of Man be lifted up"* (John 3:14).

At a time when God was upset with Israel's behavior, He chooses to show them the pathway to salvation: Place your sin upon this pole and raise it up for all to see and ask God to forgive you for sinning. God's pathway to love is simple and straightforward. Salvation comes by accepting the One who died for our sins and was raised on a tree.

Just a look at our sin upon the raised wooden pole restores life.

Yeshua reminds Nicodemus, *"anyone who is bitten can look at it and live"* (Numbers 21:8). Just a look at our sin upon the raised wooden pole restores life. He tells the Pharisee, *"that whoever believes in Him should not perish but have eternal life"* (John 3:15).

Then the most famous words spoken by Yeshua,

> *"For God so loved the world that He gave His only begotten Son, that whoever believes in Him should not perish but have everlasting life"* (John 3:16).

Nicodemus wanted to know the truth. Imagine how he would have responded to the Prophet's statement. Yeshua uses the Hebrew word *yachid*, meaning only begotten son. This was the same word God used to refer to Isaac, Abraham's only son, given in fulfillment of God's promise to Abraham's barren wife Sarah during the later days of their lives.

Nicodemus knew this term, *yachid*. All Israel knew a ram caught in the thorns of the nearby thicket would become the substitutionary sacrifice for Isaac. God did not have Isaac sacrificed. The Lord just wanted to know if Abraham's faith was strong enough to be willing to lay every claim to the future of his family on the altar by sacrificing his only son. *"Do not lay a hand on the boy,"* he [God] *said. "Do not do anything to him. Now I know that you fear God, because you have not withheld from me your son, your only son"* (Genesis 22:12).

If Nicodemus wanted to know if Yeshua was the Messiah, there would have been little room for doubt after this conversation. Yeshua made it clear, *"For God did not send His Son into the world to condemn the world, but that the world through Him might be saved"*

(John 3:17). Yeshua was showing Nicodemus that he was talking to God's only begotten Son!

Yeshua was not condemning the Sanhedrin for sinning. He was demonstrating how those who sin could be forgiven. For the Jews of that day this revelation was stunning. This was an unmistakable confirmation of Nicodemus' statement: *"Rabbi, we know that You are a teacher come from God; for no one can do these signs that You do unless God is with him."*

We are no different from Nicodemus. Having walked in sin throughout our lives, it is mind-boggling to think that the confession of faith in Yeshua is the pathway to freedom. The picture of *"the wind blows where it wishes"* tells us of the unencumbered life of someone born of the Holy Spirit. Such freedom seems unimaginable, but it is God's gift to us.

In the same way Yeshua demonstrates fishing for humanity. The Lord prepared Israel by foreshadowing the lifting of the serpent in the wilderness. In so doing, He shows us His blueprint for salvation.

> *Then they journeyed from Mount Hor by the Way of the Red Sea, to go around the land of Edom; and the soul of the people became very discouraged on the way. And the people spoke against God and against Moses: "Why have you brought us up out of Egypt to die in the wilderness? For there is no food and no water, and our soul loathes this worthless bread." So the Lord sent fiery serpents among the people, and they bit the people; and many of the people of Israel died. Therefore the people came to Moses, and said, "We have sinned, for we have spoken against the Lord and against you; pray to the Lord that He take away the serpents from us." So Moses prayed for the people. Then the Lord said to Moses, "Make a fiery serpent, and set it on a pole; and it shall be that everyone who is bitten, when he looks at it, shall live." So Moses made a bronze serpent, and put it on a pole; and so it was, if a serpent had bitten anyone, when he looked at the bronze serpent, he lived* (Numbers 21:4-9).

God knows about our proclivity to sin. Our heavenly Father knows that it will take a submitted heart to change our ways to His ways. Likewise, fishing is easy, but it takes much preparation. God is the One who completes the process of catching a fish. Causing fish to take a hook or enter a net is not our part. That's God's business. This is what God offers. And He uses fishing to demonstrate His offer of unconditional love.

For many, the gospel seems too easy. This begs the question, "Why would a loving God make receiving His love difficult?" The clear answer, "It's not difficult!" In fact, God gave us His written Word—the Bible—so we can recount these stories to strengthen our own faith and to facilitate sharing our faith with others. Fishing is easy.

Knowing this story about Nicodemus, it is understandable that this Pharisee cautions his colleagues, *"Does our law judge a man before it hears him and knows what he is doing?"* (John 7:51). And in a supreme act of reverence, he honors the crucified Lord by bringing a hundred pounds of myrrh and aloe and binds Yeshua's body with strips of linen containing these spices (John 19:38-39). Note: Not all of Israel's leaders resisted Yeshua. The most devout were the most sensitive to Jesus.

A Fish Pays Tax

When Peter and Yeshua returned to Capernaum, in Matthew chapter 17, the collectors of the Temple tax interrogate Peter as to his intention to comply. Speaking for Yeshua, Peter informs them that his Teacher pays this tax. Yeshua uses this occasion to take Peter into deep waters spiritually.

Peter returns to his house. Yeshua, knowing what concerns the disciple, brings up the subject of the Temple tax dilemma before Peter even mentions the subject. Yeshua wants Peter's opinion on who should be subject to such taxes. In a brief discussion, Yeshua asks Peter, *"What do you think, Simon? From whom do the kings of the earth take customs or taxes, from their sons or from strangers?"* Peter *said to Him, "From strangers"* (Matthew 17:25-26). But Yeshua takes a humble route. Instead of creating controversy by claiming His unique standing as God's Son, therefore not being subject to tax on the Lord's tabernacle—the obvious conclusion to the question Yeshua has put before Peter—Yeshua decides to pay the tax.

Instead of instructing Peter to pay this tax, which every Jewish person was required to give according to Exodus 30:13 as a *"ransom for his soul to Adonai,"* Yeshua makes an unexpected gesture. He decides to pay this price for Peter. The Lord determines to fulfill the law's requirements by giving out of His own resources.

Here is a foreshadowing of deep significance. The Temple tax allowed everyone over 20 years of age to enter the Tabernacle of God. Yeshua shows Peter that, when a disciple of God is serving his Master, it is the Master Himself who allows entry to the Father's house. Just as Yeshua pays the price for our sin, that payment also guarantees our access into the Kingdom of God. Hallelujah!

Gaining access to God is a supernatural event. And so, Yeshua takes Peter into the supernatural realm to foot the bill. The impossibility of Yeshua's instructions give all pause about the lengths our Savior will go to make sure we have an eternal relationship with God.

Yeshua's method of honoring the requirement to pay this tax, as instructed in Leviticus, takes Peter back out to the Sea of Galilee. He voices a remarkable request, *"Go to the sea, cast in a hook, and take the fish that comes up first. And when you have opened its mouth, you will find a piece of money; take that and give it to them for Me and you."* The verses in Matthew 17:24-27 end on this quotation. But our brains continue in full gear. Just how is it that Yeshua can make sure that a certain fish in the Sea of Galilee will take that hook? And what is mind-boggling is the coin in its mouth!

That's a whole lot of trouble to go through to pay a half-shekel fee for two men. There is no description of Peter doing so, but the implication is crystal clear. Of course Peter went fishing. Wouldn't you?

Wouldn't you want to catch that fish and find that coin? Wouldn't you test God to see if He would fulfill what He promised, as unlikely and farfetched a promise as He was making for you? I know I would.

Yeshua paid the price for Peter, and He paid the price for you and me. But we, like Peter, still have to go fishing to get the reward. Peter was thinking about the Temple tax. In light of what we have garnered from God, we now know Yeshua paid far more than the tax, He paid off the ransom for our souls!

Fishing with a Ministry Mindset

> *Then Jesus came to them and said, "All authority in heaven and on earth has been given to me. Therefore **go and make disciples of all nations**, baptizing them in the name of the Father and of the Son and of the Holy Spirit, and teaching them to obey everything I have commanded you. And surely **I am with you always, to the very end of the age**"* (Matthew 28:18-20).

Yeshua empowered us to do what He did—to use the same authority God gave to Him. And what are we to do with this awesome gift of God's authority? God wants us to go and make disciples of all nations. If you will, to be fishers of men.

The newborn disciples released into the world in those first days caused a virtual explosion in church membership. Sitting in the twenty-first century, we overlook that this was accomplished without the aid of the New Testament. Those Scriptures wouldn't appear until decades after the death of Yeshua.

Think of it: no phones and no photos; no electronics and no engines; no newspapers and no newscasts. Nevertheless, the early church grabbed the attention of the known world and the good news spread like wildfire. And wild it was; tens of thousands came to faith. What made this so fascinating is that virtually every person coming to faith was Jewish.

God chose Shavuot (celebrating God's gift of the Torah to Moses on Mount Sinai) to pour out His Holy Spirit on faithful Jewish believers assembled for prayer in an upper room in Jerusalem. (The Torah or Pentateuch formed the first five books of our Bible, referred to as Law or Instruction.) Pentecost falls fifty days after Passover, to coincide precisely with the Jewish feast of Shavuot. Every devout Jewish male would have been present in the City of David. It was no accident that God stipulated this moment to ignite His church.

Supernaturally, God poured out His miraculous love on an unsuspecting group of Jews who had joined a band of fishermen to pray. Time stood still. Calendars were reset. Ever since that sacred instant, life on our planet has never been the same.

A Whole New Paradigm

The master of the universe is not concerned about our ability to fish. He wants to know what we are fishing for and why we need to catch it. If we aren't fishing for the right reason, the catch will be sparse. Or in the case of Luke 5 and John 21, there won't be any fish at all until we submit to His sovereign plan for our life.

> *Unless the Lord builds the house, they labor in vain who build it* (Psalm 127:1).

God often frustrates our best-laid plans. Our best isn't good enough if it doesn't align with divine purposes. That's hard for us to accept. Throughout our life we are taught that doing our best is the swiftest path to success. So we conclude that our best efforts must be the blueprint to success.

"Don't mistake speed for distance."

Sometimes we are confused and we decide that doing our best is the same as doing things as unto the Lord. Certainly God wants us to do our best. However, our success is going to be measured by our proximity to God's will, not how hard we try or how fast we think we can achieve our goals. If we haven't aligned ourselves with His will, our self-designated ideas will take us in a different direction than God's desired destination. As I like to say, "Don't mistake speed for distance."

We must do all things as unto the Lord as a demonstration of our faith. But doing all things as unto the Lord requires a much deeper look at our actions than we have come to expect. Divine blueprints incorporate far, far more than we usually consider. God's plans for success diverges from ours. God is about building character. A person's best doesn't accrue much favor with God if our motivation doesn't honor His divine design.

Chapter 10

There Will Be a Catch

Empty Nets

Despite the fact that most of the disciples are fishermen and that Yeshua says He will make His followers "fishers of men," there are only these two instances in the Holy Scriptures where we experience Yeshua overtly teaching the fishermen how to fish. And on both occasions the nets are empty. A closer look reveals much.

The bookends of Jesus' earthly walk with His disciples are fashioned by fishing. From the stem to stern, fishing with Jesus is an inescapable call to all. When Jesus first encounters His disciples and asks them to follow Him, they are repairing their nets. Following Yeshua's crucifixion, Peter thinks all is said and done. Returning to the Sea of Galilee, he reverts to his previous lifestyle. The other fishermen, upon hearing Peter is going fishing, join in.

This decision was not without impetus. Recall that after His resurrection and visits to the upper room, Yeshua passes along word that He will meet His saints, and specifically Peter, at the Sea of Galilee. Knowing the Son of Man is always true to His word, the disciples are anticipating another divine visitation.

Fishing is an honorable, workingman's vocation. It's tough, honest labor. It feeds the masses. The hours are demanding. The hauling and maintenance take their toll. Fishing the Sea of Tiberius (another term for "Galilee") is not work for the lily-livered. This body of water is large and can be quite treacherous.

Peter is the picture of a weathered fisherman. He's a natural born leader, accustomed to having men follow him. He's atop the pecking order aboard his craft. The captain and his compatriots are about to get their second, and definitive, course in catching. At both episodes Jesus teaches them much more than how to catch fish. Peter will be severely tested on both occasions and is completely undone. And who wouldn't be disheveled? The Lord intentionally uses these miraculous events to orchestrate His absolute authority and mastery over His creation.

At his first encounter with the twelve, upon emerging from the wilderness, Jesus prays to His Father for guidance. The next morning He obediently selects those He will teach to lead—to become fishers of men. He starts with empty nets. And at the Sea of Galilee the disciples are confounded again—empty nets.

As the church enters hard times, may we learn to lean on the Lord and not on our own talents. He will supply all our needs. Empty nets teach us our total reliance on God.

Offering Our Livelihood

When Jesus first meets Peter, the fishing boats have already been returned to the shore with nothing to show for their day's labor. The fishermen are cleaning their nets. A large crowd, who hungered to hear him speak, surround the Man of Miracles (Luke 5:1-11).

Realizing that a boat positioned a few yards offshore will allow His voice to carry over the water, Jesus asks to use Peter's fishing vessel—a fisherman's most prized possession. It's not clear whether Peter knew why Jesus wanted the boat, but he graciously agrees. Jesus delivers His message to the multitude, then turns to Peter and instructs him to set out his nets once again.

This request leads to the defining moment of Peter's life. Jesus directs him to *"Launch out into the deep and let down your nets for a catch.*" Peter is perturbed. Jesus has no upbringing to qualify him for fishing. The Prophet has stepped over the line of propriety.

The big fisherman had already complied by granting Jesus the use of his boat. Jesus got what he asked for. The audience received the message. Everything looked to be in order. It was time to call it a day and go home. Peter protests, *"Master, we have toiled all night and caught nothing."*

Peter addresses Jesus as *"Master."* This helps to explain why he complies with the request.

Peter and his partners have just heard this Wise Man speak, and assuredly touch the hearts of all gathered. To resist is futile. *"Nevertheless at your word I will let down the net."*

The future apostle hasn't the foggiest idea that his obedience to the Lord's directive will reconfigure his life forever. The allegorical reference *"into the deep"* is applicable on numerous levels. Peter is literally over his head. What happens next unmistakably demonstrates Jesus' mastery over nature.

Jesus doesn't just tell Peter to go fishing, or at least not specifically so. His statement reflects supreme confidence in the perceived outcome. There's nary a hint of the possibility of failure. Nor is there merely the likelihood of getting something in the net; rather the Lord's declaration carries an assured result—*there will be a catch.*

As this episode is recounted, it's clear Peter and his friends are totally unprepared to receive an unprecedented haul of fish. The harvest is on such a scale that Peter's ship, as well as another summoned to assist, start to sink as they try to manage the bounty.

It's all too much for Peter. Realizing he's entirely unworthy of God's favor, Peter is virtually drowning in his own depravity. He is in desperate need of Jesus. Peter is a man who is used to having things done his own way. Nevertheless, God is not going to allow that to happen. Peter encounters his own pride face to face. He's overwhelmed that God, despite his obvious flaws, would want to use him.

This is surely a pictorial preview of the end times harvest of souls. The church is sorely unprepared for the vast numbers to come. We will not only need each other's boats and deck hands, we will be overwhelmed with the scale of ministry we are called to perform.

Jethro instructed Moses about effective ministerial outreach for the same reasons. Unless we are willing to adopt the model given by Yeshua, the church community that resists unification will sink under the weight of the calling of discipleship.

Are you ready for the coming catch?

Goldfish Heaven

Catch and release brings to mind recreational fly-fishing on a hidden bend of whitewater in the Rocky Mountains with a peanut butter and jelly sandwich tucked into my backpack. It's one of the finest sports on God's green earth. Fresh air. A healthy hike. Peace and quiet. Beautiful scenery. Getting in touch with yourself and your surroundings. Nothing like it.

Failing the life-and-death struggle, there comes an unexpected release. In my own world I have "saved" a few fish. There's a small pond with a waterfall in my backyard that broadcasts the music of falling water. Over the years I've released a few dozen goldfish from the local pet store into that shallow pool.

These are feeder fish, destined to be lunch for some turtle or fellow reptile. A fortunate few may make it to a small fishbowl or aquarium on some youngster's dresser. These young swimmers are an inch or two long and only cost a dime. They are bred and marked for an early demise. I doubt if any can imagine a private pond with fellow finned friends.

I'm giving them a second chance. Even in the relative safety of my backyard there are hazards—cats, raccoons, even a great blue heron has come to dine on my wet pets. Fortunately, our dog Sadie shoos them away. The pond itself presents its own hazards as some fish are inevitably drawn into the screen and filter immediately in front of the pump. And the cold takes its toll. However, a few have lasted several years and grown to about four inches. I'm especially proud of these savvy survivors.

I chuckle whenever I'm buying a bunch to replenish my supply. The fish don't know that this particular trapping ends in freedom. Once the pet store employee dips his net into the fish tank, the fish scurry every which way to avoid capture. I tell them through the aquarium glass that this is the one time when it pays great dividends to get caught, but they can't see their reward. Understandably, they are desperate to escape the snare. They sense danger and fear for their future.

We understand their resistance, because the net is intimidating. Leaving the water represents certain death. However, this transfer from death to new life is the way the Kingdom of God operates. Viewing the alternative of being a lizard's lunch, my pond represents freedom for young goldfish. They have a benevolent overseer and are supplied with all their needs. Of course, they would be well-advised to learn the survival skills that allow them to exist even in protected environments. Their only responsibility is to dine on the healthy algae that abounds, and live happy lives.

I wonder if these goldfish, once they are released into my pond, think they're in Heaven?

Part III

Going Deep

Chapter 11

The Good Shepherd

Protecting Your Sheep

As evening approaches, a shepherd locates cover for his sheep. He finds a cave or an outcropping of rocks that offers protection for his flock from inclement weather and defends them from dangerous predators. He wisely adds sturdy branches and other natural barriers to seal off access to his precious livestock. As night falls he beds down across the shelter entry to prevent his sheep from escaping or unwelcome intruders from sneaking inside.

Every shepherd must take the role of defending his flock seriously. There are a great many forces that want to take advantage of sheep. While many pastors pride themselves on being very wary, such a defensive mindset can easily take on a life of its own. This protective instinct can draw a leader into a hidden snare of our enemy. That trap is the possessiveness that comes with being overly protective of human sheep. The result of being too restrictive inhibits the expansion of God's Kingdom.

Overcautious pastors cling too tightly to their gifted followers. (Note: All who follow Yeshua are gifted by Him.) This can stifle and prevent the members of their flock from stepping outside the so-called "protective" confines of church into the world of their ministry callings. But that's exactly where God has called us to go.

This chronic error has become so widespread that it affects a vast number of Western churches. In defense of pastors, let's remember that our world can be a risky place. Nevertheless, our job is to prepare saints to serve in the battlefield. We are directing our constituents to use the church as a launching pad for ministerial outreach. For those pastors who do encourage and send their sheep out to engage our world, I applaud your vision to equip the saints. Your pond will flourish. Your fish will enjoy abundant life and see God's miracles firsthand.

Nonetheless, there is a deeply significant situation that underlies the reason pastors are reluctant to release. The cause is not readily apparent, as we have gradually become complacent in current church culture. Our congregations have become adaptive to a lukewarm liquid that is being slowly heated to the boiling point. We have to face the fact that the church has lost much of its traction in the Western world. The roots of this problem need to be exposed to the light of day and pulled out so we get back to the river. Just one hop and we're released!

We have to face the fact that the church has lost much of its traction in the Western world.

We need to take a look at the misperceptions of pastors. May this urge us to pray more fervently for the ones who are willing to teach, restore, and kneel before His throne of grace on our behalf. The enemy has been tearing up the vine.

The Shepherd's Role

How can the Kingdom of God advance by restraining the release of gifted leaders? How will we impact our surrounding world?

The sad result of misunderstanding a shepherd's proper role is that we have come to use the label of "covering our sheep" in an overly restrictive mode. The fivefold offices of apostle, prophet, evangelist, pastor, and teacher were given to us to effectively build up believers, so all would use their gifts and talents in outreach and ministry. Once disciples are properly prepped, we need to be ready to set free those desiring to actively minister outside the confines of the sanctuary. But this cannot happen unless we release believers into their callings.

Unfortunately, most clergy respond to the fivefold ministry titles by considering the width and breadth of their own mantle. Yet the following verses point to the *purposes* of ministry, more so than to positions of management. The Word of God spells this out for us in Ephesians 4:11-13. These positions are designated for the edification of the body, that we would perform good works, as God has ordained for all believers.

> *And He Himself gave some to be apostles, some prophets, some evangelists, and some pastors and teachers,* **for the equipping of the saints for the work of ministry, for the edifying of the body of Christ**, *till we all come to the unity of the faith and of the knowledge of the Son of God, to a perfect man, to the measure of the stature of the fullness of Christ;*

Too often the instructions on how to wear the mantle for church leadership entrap us. It's easy to fall prey to this deception, neglecting God's intended result. Failing to understand God's designated role—*for the edifying of the body of Christ*—for ministry causes the church to disempower its most potent weapon—its membership. The Lord is telling us that through unity and knowledge of His Son we become more like Yeshua, the One whom God sent.

To engage in the proper functioning of these essential offices, pastors need to be equipped to release their leaders, just as these leaders are being equipped by these same pastors in anticipation of beginning their future ministries.

Instead of equipping people to attain mature (perfect) knowledge, we choose to modify our understanding for ministry by directing others to come under our own brand of leadership. We are still treating the sheep, including potential shepherds, as if they will not be safe unless they remain under our own covering. Discipleship can become sidetracked into a program for teaching in classrooms with little emphasis on sending the saints into the world. Of course we need the full counsel of God, but it is no coincidence that the fastest growing churches in the world focus on outreach. Nevertheless, we are still cognizant that outreach alone is not the simple solution for a healthy body.

The need for future leaders who haven't been released and the diminishing numbers in church growth are closely linked. When gifted elders and lay leaders are constrained, the church pays a price. At some point there comes the inevitable pushback from even the most devout church staff.

Those same members, the ones pastors have come to lean on through windstorms and high seas, decide to protest. This often comes as a shock, because the mature ones, those who have stood closely by their shepherds through the rough weather of church growth and have received invaluable training, will suddenly leave the church or instigate a split. Shepherds feel abandoned and underappreciated by their cohorts without acknowledging their own complicity in initiating their departure.

We often refer to these individuals as "rebellious." We think back on all the energy expended to pour ourselves into their lives. We perform marriages and funerals; our kids play on the same sports teams; we carpool for school, etc. Yes, there are sheep who don't appreciate the sacrifice of shepherds. But the lack of church growth is too often the result of inflexibility and insensitivity of leaders. Pastors need to widen their vision.

When gifted followers aren't given a voice, even after proving themselves through trials and tribulations, a day will come when they need to make a shift. Even our own children need to leave home when they mature. It's no different with our church children. When they grow up, we need to cut the apron strings.

Leaders need to lead, or they'll find another outlet for their talents. Pastors with a Kingdom mindset seek these chosen ones to help them pave the pathway toward their destiny. That pathway, with extremely few exceptions, will lead them outside their home assembly. Perhaps down the road some will return to the roost, but we all reach a point where we need to flap our wings and wiggle our fins.

When a leader leaves a church without approval, the senior pastor commonly feels betrayed by the very sheep he has taught to become mature. A misdirected model that mimics the corporate culture of the Western world entices our up-and-coming disciples to stay onboard for far too long, if not indefinitely.

When the day finally arrives for a leader to step out into his or her chosen ministry, an immature administrator may misinterpret this move toward independence as disobedience. Healthy sheep need to be moved regularly to find greener pastures. Wise shepherds rotate their flocks to new fields to prevent overgrazing. These sheep will flourish as they have a steady diet of fresh greens and extra exercise to boot. This also avoids overgrazing, so grasses swiftly recover, permitting healthier foliage for the next return of the flock.

Of course there are distinguishable cases of disobedience. We must emphasize that we don't want to make the error of sending out saints before they are ready. In any organization some want to usurp positions of authority prematurely, so the desire to lead must be tempered with wisdom, maturity, and proper timing. Let's not lose sight of our goal—to release the sheep.

The beauty of Yeshua's discipling process is that He sends out the saints as a foundational part of their instruction. As a young believer receives instruction from a mature person of faith, it's easy to recognize his or her progress. The hands-on approach to ministry is the swiftest and most effective method of learning. Discipling that employs a philosophy of close contact creates opportunities to gauge the growth of new disciples. Pastors would do well to discern those ready to be released. And certainly we must be humble enough to see our own vulnerability before judging our sheep.

Being under the cover of pastoral care is essential for accountability and proper nurturing. But holding back the next generation of conquerors delays the church of Yeshua HaMashiach from fulfilling its destiny to reach as many as possible with the Good News.

The thinking that is ingrained in many Western churches is for building bigger and bigger churches. Pastors ponder, "How can we build a big church if our best leaders leave?" This is not a condemnation of large churches. Large churches are potential powerhouses to change cities and nations. This is a cautionary word that encourages us to identify, train, and release the saints into their highest calling, wherever that may take them, both inside and outside of their home assembly.

As maturing leaders are released, younger, eager saints will have the opportunity to move up in the ranks. This encourages growth, teamwork, and participation.

If a church has proper understanding and application of the Word of God, it may grow rapidly. Our concern is to utilize Jesus' model of discipleship, so the church grows properly by raising up its best leaders—to serve both inside and outside the four walls. As maturing leaders are released, younger, eager saints will have the opportunity to move up in the ranks. This encourages growth, teamwork, and participation. What church wouldn't want that outcome?

Setting the Sheep Out to Pasture

How could shepherds have missed this calling to release our disciples? Returning to the original image for a protective covering, the answer is not difficult to discern—we're prone to overlook the time of day. Shelter is supposed to be sought during darkness, not while the sun shines. Of course there are times when the weather is threatening and we need to take cover for a short spell. However, during daylight hours we have to let the sheep out of the pen.

A strong flock thrives by foraging and finding fresh grass. God designed sheep to be outdoors on the hillsides. The same is true for the church. A vibrant, robust church is in constant contact with its surrounding environs because the flock of believers is infiltrating their community, their mission field. This outreach to our local region and the world beyond is the pathway over which our Lord wants us to reach, touch, and connect with humanity.

The same holds true for raising healthy fish. They need pure water. Fresh water moves and breathes as it rolls over rocks and gets tossed by wind and waves. Open water affords mobility, sunlight, and rain. Fish from swiftly moving streams and seas are strong. They are ready to respond to life's challenges.

The gates of hell do not prevail over the Kingdom of God. In other words, the enemy cannot prevent us from taking the ground the Lord has given us to conquer. Those gates were never intended to confine the saints of God, furthermore, they are placed in front of our foe's turf, not ours. We will not conquer our enemy by staying inside gated ponds and pastures. Furthermore, we are told that our enemy can't hold us back when we move in the power and authority of the living God. A church that truly impacts its neighborhood passes through such gates.

Saints need to be encouraged to seek good pastures. Failing to do so risks restraining our potential leaders. If they don't feel the freedom to grow and expand their own tent pegs, dynamic candidates will soon have one eye on the exit. Strong leaders are ideal for creating powerful infrastructure inside a large church, but that season should not be overextended. Remember, over time, even our staunchest allies begin to seek a place to break out and to respond to the calling to evangelize and to build his or her ministry.

If these future leaders do "escape" stagnant waters, what type of church have they been taught to build? The model they've experienced reinforces a flawed discipleship program that trains those with apostolic gifts to hold onto leaders too tightly; failing to return them to the flowing waters. A most intriguing tendency of human behavior is our repetition of the errors of our predecessors.

This pattern continues, even when we know that we have been misguided. Thus the cycle of overbearing leadership continues, along with the trap that insists on blind loyalty as the sign of a mature saint. Too many gifted ones won't make the leap because we've held them back.

Releasing Your Sheep

The principle of release is directly connected to the Sabbath. The seventh day of the week and the seventh year of a cycle are appointed times of rest. This text is being penned during a "Shmitah" year, or Sabbath year of release. This principle is foundational to healthy living. Rest and release are inextricably combined. In fact, to ignore our need for rest is itself an act of disobedience.

We have moved away from rest. Unlike the days of my youth, stores are open on Sundays. It's more and more difficult to find exceptions. In our frantic pace to accomplish more, we have developed tools that don't take a Sabbath. Unlike oxen, computers can run continuously. I do find it ironic that one of the most effective techniques for troubleshooting my computer is to shut it down, if you will, to push "reset." Quite often an "electronic Sabbath" fixes the problem.

So even the item that makes it easiest to avoid taking a true Sabbath requires "rest." The idea of overload is not just for breathing creatures. This concept extends to electronics, machinery, and equipment. Equipping saints for release requires the rest period where God restores and redirects our paths. How interesting that this applies for both animate and inanimate realms of existence.

Overlooking rest is not a shortcut to greater productivity. Overworking leads to loss of efficiency and burnout. Without proper rest we are more susceptible to disease, accidents, and reduced creativity. For all the creature comforts we can now enjoy on our Sabbath day, there is not and never will be a substitute for rest.

And this rest is essential for preparing and softening our hearts. With all the busyness of our lives, it is not possible to fully hear from God until we shut the engine down. Yeshua modeled this, as He would go off alone to quiet places. Sometimes He was gone all night. If the King of glory needed to do this, we know we need to emulate our Master.

When the Lord gave His Commandments to Moses on Mount Sinai, He reminded Israel that even our Creator took the seventh day off. To further prove His point, God waited for seven sevens of days before giving us the Torah, His instructions for living a life that honors Him. It's no accident that Shavuot, the giving of the law, signified the appointed time for all of Israel to come to the Temple on Mount Zion to celebrate this occasion. Nor is it merely a coincidence that this was exactly the hour when the Holy Spirit came down to touch Yeshua's chosen ones with tongues of fire.

On that day of Shavuot, in obedience to God's commandment, the City of Jerusalem was swollen with devout Jews. Israel worshiped God as they rested in Him. And God honored their rest by releasing the very presence of His being to continue the ministry of Yeshua. God sent us His Son from the realm of His Majestic Glory. After receiving Yeshua back into Heaven, God released His Majestic Glory back on earth in the form of His *Ruach HaKodesh* (The Holy Spirit) to fill and fulfill our lives.

Unquestionably, God demonstrates the necessity for release. The timing was precisely, sovereignly predetermined to confirm Yeshua's ministry to His disciples and to all of Israel. The Shmitah, the appointed Sabbath hour, day, and year for His release, is perfect. The heavens were aligned from the moment of creation to give us the indelible picture of a Father's love for His Son. We can only praise and thank Him for doing so. As we rest in Him, He does the rest.

Releasing the 99

Just as the Lord keeps His flock in order, many shepherds with protective instincts long to hold their sheep close. However, the parable of Luke 15 focuses on a single lost sheep that has gone astray. Here Yeshua decides to release the flock.

As the shepherd goes looking for his one lost sheep he doesn't corral his livestock. Luke 15:4 tells us that a shepherd has 100 sheep, but loses one. So where does he leave the other 99 sheep? Out in the open field! Some Bible translations use hills, mountains, or wilderness—in direct contrast to the safety of a sheltered corral.

> *What man of you, having a hundred sheep, if he loses one of them, does not leave the ninety-nine in the wilderness, and go after the one which is lost until he finds it?*

The Lord trusts His sheep to know how to forage. Over time they have learned how to stay safe in unrestricted environments. The shepherd's attention is centered on the one in trouble. The rest of the sheep are doing what they do best—grazing out in wide-open spaces.

An example of compassion in action is *FIAT (Faith Initiative Against Trafficking)* started as a gathering of Los Angeles based churches and individuals who have been called to fight human trafficking. They train and encourage believers to get actively involved in confronting slavery. For more information about this most commendable outreach, please turn to the Noteworthy Ketches in the back of the book.

Keeping our flock bottled up has serious consequences. It stifles church growth and doesn't allow the sheep to graze and stay healthy. Sheep need space to roam in order to locate adequate fresh feed. They feel naturally protected in a herd. When an errant sheep strays, the shepherd need only concerning himself with retrieving the disobedient one.

> ***Yeshua taught us the principle that after we catch a fish and get it cleaned up, we need to put it back into the River of Life!***

Sheep stay healthiest when they are released to forage. That's why Yeshua taught us the principle that after we catch a fish and get it cleaned up, we need to put it back into the River of Life!

The Celebration of Release

As new leaders step out into fields of ministry, existing church leadership can use this point of release as a celebration of their skills. Instead of taking such departures as some type of personal rejection, such a release signifies a graduation into higher callings and more influential ministry. This is the best sign of healthy church growth.

Church growth seminars traditionally focus on established pastors expanding preexisting churches. Extending outreach and church planting are relegated to different seminars. Fortunately there are some very encouraging signs new trends are germinating for up-and-coming leaders. This is what our Lord encouraged us to accomplish.

The shift into the classification of "nondenominational" churches indicates the desire for leaders to break out of restrictive molds. While this is not always a condemnation of denominations, it does reflect the natural desire for leaders to blaze new trails in building the Kingdom of Heaven.

We are the church of Jesus the Christ. It's not our church. It's His church. We are His body and He is the Head of the church. The body cannot fulfill its calling if it is not releasing leaders. Failure to recognize and release those who are ready causes much division. This stand is in stark contrast to our Lord's directive. Yeshua taught His fishermen how to multiply. That's how we become fishers of men.

Chapter 12

Good Works, Good Boat, Good Crew

Communication

Practicing ministry requires a high level of communication. Most church leaders are accomplished communicators. Believers are passionate about their faith. Still the headcount in the Kingdom of Heaven wanes. Where's the disconnect?

Wisely, we continually emphasize prayer as the best way to communicate with God. In prayer we open up a two-way conversation with God. During this time of communion we gain divine insight on both Heaven and earth. Stop and think about it. We are allowed to speak to the Ancient of Days. He wants to know what's on our hearts and minds. He cares that much about us.

As remarkable as it is for us to gain God's ear, it's nothing compared to the fact that He wants our ears! God speaks to us. In fact, God is always speaking to us. The reason we pray is so we can speak to Him, as well as to hear what He has to say. Knowing this, it's incredible that more people don't pray more often.

> *Indeed, he who watches over Israel will neither slumber nor sleep* (Psalm 121:4 NIV).

> *Call to Me and I will answer you, and show you great and mighty things* (Jeremiah 33:3).
>
> *...the Lord...will never leave you or forsake you* (Deuteronomy 31:6 NIV).

We can go on with the verses that prove God wants to be close to us. But if we are not listening for His guidance, we won't hear Him. If we are preoccupied with our own lives, we're too busy for Him. If we have our own agendas, we won't respond to His requests.

If we are spending a lot of time in prayer, then the Lord will be greatly pleased by our desire to draw close to Him. And most assuredly our Savior will have particular tasks that He will ask us to perform. There's a serious gap if a person claims to have a close relationship with the God of all creation but doesn't take the time to intercede and minister to those in need.

Reaching out to those near and far, *Hosanna Broadcasting Network* broadcasts the gospel by uniting believers around the world and bringing the message of salvation to those most difficult to access. For more information about HBN, turn to Noteworthy Ketches in the back of the book.

Either we aren't really praying; or we are speaking, but not listening to God; or we have decided we don't have time; or we don't want to do what God is asking us to do. God has things He wants us to do. Kingdom living is not a passive, lukewarm walk of faith. God doesn't dish out *dunamis,* then expect us to stay distant.

As mentioned in Chapter 3 and is worth repeating, Galatians 6:10 cuts to the marrow of the matter: *"Therefore, as we have opportunity, let us do good to all, especially to those who are of the household of faith."* This is our Lord's way of unifying us by joining arms and demonstrating our love for Him in the way we do good. To whatever degree we hold back on partnering with our brothers and sisters in the faith is a reflection of the depth of our walk with God.

Good Works

We are overwhelmed by the faith of prayer warriors and the gifts of our worship teams. They definitely hunger to know God's heart. And if we know what is in God's heart, then certainly it will show up in how we treat others. The gospel calls for good works. Most churches teach the importance of helping our neighbors and our friends. Our prayers and worship are pleasing incense. So where's the fruit?

As we study the Great Commission of Matthew 28, we are urged to *"Go and make disciples."* Believers are very intentional in sharing the Good News. So where are the ones who should be filling the pews?

I recall my elementary school days with "Show and Tell." We would "show" the class something of interest, then we would "tell" everyone about it. Have we been "telling" the world the good news, but not "showing" our good works to accompany our message?

Believers worship and call upon the Lord. Worship teams take us to the throne of grace and seek God's face. Still the church is not flourishing in America. Time to get on our faces. We need a breakthrough.

> *The Spirit of America, a nation founded on godly principles by our God-fearing founders, is malnourished. How could this happen?*

Prayer and worship are absolute necessities and we claim to be doing these things; however, the Spirit of America, a nation founded on godly principles by our God-fearing founders, is malnourished. How could this happen here?

I expect every church leader out there will want to defend some, if not all of his or her activities. But I am asking you, what's missing? Are we humble enough to look at our own shortcomings? Are we wise enough to realize that the church is culpable? Are we willing to admit the answer lies inside, not outside the church?

God gave us complete authority. If things aren't right, we can't blame our society, our culture, our government, our economy, our teachers, our leaders, our bosses, our families, or anything else. As the Lord sent His angel and spoke to Gideon: *"And the Angel of the Lord appeared to him, and said to him, 'The Lord is with you, you mighty man of valor!'"* (Judges 6:12).

We don't lack anything except the conviction that comes with real faith. And frankly, the resistance we are encountering in the United States is nothing compared to what goes on in many nations. And still, God will have His way and His church will flourish and accomplish His desires.

Good works happen as soon as we decide to do them. Jesus released us. We've got His permission. There is nothing, I repeat, nothing, holding us back from doing what we've always wanted to do. Hebrews 10:24 (NIV) provides inspiration: *"And let us consider how we may spur one another on toward love and good deeds."*

Titles

While we claim to be following our King's clear instructions, our style of fishing seldom matches the method taught and exemplified by Yeshua. We've missed His boat!

We have mentioned communication, outreach, prayer, and worship. A close look at these specific activities gives us a better view of the attributes of our character. By adopting the culture of the West, the church has imported some corporate guidelines that are causing confusion.

We have made a serious miscalculation in believing that secular titles will achieve the same results inside the church as they do in the marketplace. Secular titles usually describe position and stature within an organization. Kingdom titles inform us of behaviors. There is a vast difference between these labels. We expect corporate motivation will achieve the same results inside the church as it does in the profit-centered world.

Yeshua had to explain to His followers that the process of fishing for men, while employing much of the same philosophy in the Kingdom as on the Sea of Galilee, requires a better understanding of human strengths and weaknesses. When Yeshua told His disciples that He would make them fishers of men, He informed them that there was going to be a new way to fish. The challenges were going to be different.

Building the Kingdom of God would require a fresh approach. So Yeshua had to teach His fishermen about the spiritual realm. He had to show His disciples about the strongholds of the enemy. He knew that an effective fishing vessel is the by-product of a well-trained crew.

We have allowed our cultural models of leadership and organization to redefine church structure. In so doing, we have reconfigured God's blueprint for fishing. In some ways we are acting as if the church is Noah's Ark. Will there be a storm where we will wish to close all the doors and portholes? Yes, but there will also be a great revival, the greatest revival in the history of humanity. Our doors need to be open, not closed. We need to get out, not stay in.

And at the risk of offending much of the church that expects to be taken up out of the mess that is to come, I have to ask myself why it is that God would desert so many at the hour when their hearts are finally softened by circumstance. Oh yes, we can say that everyone has had their chance to hear the gospel. But then we'd miss the "show" in "Show and Tell."

Deep Sea Fishing

The Lord directs the fishermen to a head out toward the center of the sea. Going to deep waters means looking for big fish and a big catch. Big fish go deep. There's more room for big fish to maneuver out there. Large schools of fish need open waters to satisfy their appetites. You won't get a big catch from the shore.

Little fish seek out the shallows. Because they are at the lower end of the food chain, most everything out there sees small fish as lunch. Small fry need vegetation and shoreline rocks to stay hidden. Survival means safety in numbers, especially when you are small. Shelter near the shoreline is synonymous with security.

But there is a more significant aspect to fishing in specific locations. The realm of Heaven, just as the geography of earth, is divided into territories. God is sovereign over all creation, and He has separated His handiwork regionally. In Genesis He gives humanity dominion over all the earth. On earth, as in Heaven, there are boundaries. Just as big fish frequently stake out a portion of a reef, our Lord disseminates corresponding authority on land.

Fish instinctively know certain places offer protection. Schooling in the open sea and hiding in coral reefs is natural. Unprotected fish are subject to attack. The same holds true for isolated believers and congregations. Churches that become autonomously self-reliant overlook this fundamental tenet of strength. Our enemy looks for ways to separate us from the body. Let's not make it easy for him.

Our relationship with God is for our personal protection. The Lord's Prayer reminds us of this: *"Deliver us from evil"* confirms the ongoing conflict. Establishing God's authority for advancing His Kingdom can't be accomplished without the joint cooperation of other churches in our territory. Why? Because Yeshua instructed us to be united and that's what He will honor. To think that another procedure is going to yield greater success tells God you know more about fishing than He does. Why don't you ask Saint Peter to share his story about this!

Every mission and outpost needs partners to keep strong. This holds true for food, health, and social well-being, not to mention spiritual strength. Being part of a church divided into a multitude of denominations and cultures severely stifles the effectiveness of our ministries. Think about how many separate churches offer the same ministry. Most of these require volunteers to exist. We invariably find similar understaffed ministries duplicated in church after church. How many churches offer singles retreats, screen the identical broadcasts, require childcare, or trips to the ballpark? We are all fishing and competing against each other in the same shallow waters.

Just think, we could combine resources to become more effective in fulfilling our mutual needs and overcoming our shared challenges. This would alleviate undue strain on the body and avoid duplicating administrative skills that can be reallocated. Lord, help us to become one body with Yeshua as the Head.

A mature group of leaders from differing churches can provide a regional prayer covering that is more sensitive to the specific needs of our community. When elders step out in unity and take authority over a territory, the plots of our enemy are dismantled—literally. A mantle is given to those with the highest authority. By continuing on a divided path, we forfeit the spiritual authority that our Lord has granted us to bring down the hosts of wickedness over our region.

> *Continuing on a divided path, forfeits the spiritual authority that our Lord has granted us to bring down the hosts of wickedness over our region.*

When we pray and serve alongside our neighbors, we do so with an understanding of the local issues, urban challenges, city officials, and government. We know firsthand about the school board budget, the police department, the weather, the potholes on Main Street, and all the vicissitudes that define our community's ailments. There is genuine power in a unified body of believers. Such a grouping is the ideal place to appoint those with recognized leadership skills. As we take collective authority over a region, the church injects the missing stability.

> *Where there is no counsel, the people fall; but in the multitude of counselors there is safety* (Proverbs 11:14).

The Kingdom of God will be established and flourish with an intentional unity of prayer, praise, purpose, and partnership. This is what the one new man looks like. Kingdom advancement requires combining resources to take territory. Unity flows out of shared commitments to conquer our enemy's strongholds. With a unified body, we can venture onto any body of water and fish the deepest depths.

The Good Crew

A good fishing boat needs a good crew. The best fishermen are measured by the size of the catch, not the dimensions of the boat, or even the number of years they've been fishing. Look at the roles a good crew performs to be fishers of men.

Job descriptions are essential for understanding, coordination, and success. Consider how the fivefold gift of ministerial leadership is presented as previously pointed out in Ephesians 4:11, *"He Himself gave some to be apostles, some prophets, some evangelists, and some pastors and teachers."* These titles describe callings to leadership. The Lord assigns such titles as functional, much more than positional.

The Kingdom Center in Oxnard, California, exhibits a remarkable unity by bringing a collection of churches together in support of Gabriel's House to solve community problems such as transitional and emergency shelter. For more information, please turn to the Noteworthy Ketches in the back of the book.

These five roles are for the uplifting, edification, and preparation of the saints to be ministers of the gospel. Just as Yeshua teaches us to be fishers of men, we learn these techniques in order to teach others the same skills. As with fishing, ministry is an "all hands-on deck" activity.

Those serving on a fishing boat are expected to perform designated tasks, resulting in a great catch. Likewise, the callings of ministry are given to direct and coordinate our efforts, that we would be truly effective in fishing for souls. This achievement seems obvious, but attaining the ultimate goal of producing mature believers runs counter intuitive. Leadership is an art to be mastered with humility, not a title to be treasured with pride.

> *Leadership is an art to be mastered with humility, not a title to be treasured with pride.*

To believe that placing someone into a particular slot will motivate him or her follows the world's model. But honoring the heavenly goal of soul winning goes contrary to the worldview. When our job title gives us a misplaced perception of authority, we can get lured away. Our fleshly desire for recognition permits prestige to govern our decisions. This interferes with God's purpose. The Kingdom of God's objective for all these ministries is to provide service, performed with lovingkindness.

The power that flows from God's throne is exhibited through humility. Usurping authority as the means to control others is a sign of weakness and immaturity, not strength. Using position to gain leverage displays a lack of faith. The focus of mature leadership is on the needs of those individuals who make the team work. Highly effective leaders are sensitive to all the issues of life. This harmonious attitude of caring about others builds faith and cohesiveness within our team.

All of us have an awareness of a higher calling on our lives. When that opportunity comes knocking, we need to be ready. No activity can be more important to us than following God. Promotion from God does not happen prematurely. Yeshua didn't come before His disciples were ready to receive Him. As they prepared their nets, God was preparing their hearts to follow the One He was sending their way.

We think that we can follow a prescribed pathway for success. Do this and do that and everything will come together for you. Man's way teaches us to paint by numbers. God's ways require leaning on Him and allowing Him to establish the best boundaries. This is also counterintuitive. We can fish our way or God's way. Therefore, Yeshua needed to show these fishermen the difference. Fishing will never be the same once Yeshua gets hold of you.

Seldom does the Lord punish us for what we fail to do; He is patiently waiting for us to do what He has instructed us to do. God gives simple, clear instructions. Our conversations often speak of discerning God's will. But our problems are not centered on whether we *know* God's will. The real challenge we face concerns our willingness to *do* what the Lord has already asked us to do. If we study God's Word, we know God's will. Let's face it; we just resist putting it into action.

Consider the Lord telling the fishermen where to put their nets. These men thought they knew how to fish. They were fishermen by trade. Putting the nets down on the other side of the boat was simplistic, even absurd. What difference could that make?

Catching fish God's way means making others more important than ourselves. That's the attitude that awaits us on the other side of the boat. Obviously the fish could swim into their net on either side of the craft. God demonstrates that His blessings flow out of obedience. No wonder we push back against His guidance. It's tough to take on humility as an emblem of leadership.

That's why we have to be familiar with the Bible to learn proper models of behavior. The models of success in the Holy Scriptures are preceded by learning obedience, humility, and trust in the Lord of the universe. If it truly were God who is directing our paths, then why would we refuse to do what He asks?

We are all like Naaman, the Syrian commander with leprosy who sought the Hebrew prophet's divine healing. We expect bold signs and wonders to accompany our encounter with God. But the prophet Elijah didn't even bother to leave his lodge to speak with Naaman. Instead, he sends out his servant Gehazi to tell the leader to wash himself seven times in the Jordan. Look at 2 Kings chapter 5.

Naaman responds just like the rest of us. He is offended. He has just arrived at the prophet's home after a lengthy journey. His camels are laden with gifts. He's ready to make a show of it. He wants to take part in his own recovery. He expects to have a personal encounter with the prophet. If this man of God really can heal him, the story is going to make headlines in the evening news in Damascus. The general is preoccupied with curtain calls and people throwing flowers at him.

But the leprosy that afflicts Naaman won't leave unless he is humble. Notice that Elisha's instructions are received with disdain:

> *But Naaman was angered and walked away, saying, "I thought he would surely come out to me, stand and call on the Name of Adonai his God, and wave his hand over the spot and cure the tza'arat* [leprosy]. *Aren't Amanah and Pharpar, the rivers of Damascus, better than all the waters of Israel? Couldn't I wash in them and be clean?" So he turned and went away in a rage* (2 Kings 5:11-12 TLV).

Unfortunately, the church doesn't recognize its own tendency to act as Naaman. We share his concern with our position and our appearance. We expect a perceived piety is all that the Lord requires, and we are upset with the God of Israel for not multiplying our efforts to increase the number of new believers. That's our idea of the miracle of multiplication for loaves and fishes.

Our leaders need to grasp the necessary attitude about fishing before we can impart wisdom to the disciples. We *cannot* force fish into our nets. We *can* humbly thank God for His divine provision. The church has to be willing to wash in the river of God's choosing instead of our own. I submit that the Lord wants us to fish His Way, and then our nets will be full again. That requires a change in our attitude and corresponding behavior. But that makes for a good crew.

As obvious as this appears, the current condition of the church with declining memberships speaks an unavoidable statement that the church in the West is not flourishing as it has in our past. We preach the whole gospel, but we suffer when we fail to practice all of what we preach.

Chapter 13

The Spirit of America

Is there any wonder why the church in Western culture is shrinking? Superimposing our own societal designs for corporate growth on top of the grid given to us by God blurs the blueprint necessary for Kingdom-centered growth. A gospel based on love has difficulty maintaining its course under the guidance of misappropriated priorities.

Any leadership models that allow or encourage the celebrity status we admire in our corporate culture to be granted to anyone other than Messiah Yeshua will inevitably self-destruct. The charismatic gifts that we adopt and assign to leadership are meant for edifying the lay people, not those in charge. By drawing attention to a few dynamic personalities in our quest for effective churches, we not only neglect the poor and the needy, we give a misguided perception that God cares more about high profile leaders than the hungry and the lost.

Yes, we are to give honor to those worthy of honor. This verse is not for the purpose of glorifying humankind. We are to give honor based upon the way a leader or individual has glorified God in his or her life. This does not diminish the value of the recipient's efforts and dedication; it simply keeps us aligned with the source of the gifts that we have the privilege of distributing. Hard work is to be rewarded, but never at the expense of our standing with God.

Knowing this, we realize why church growth has been stifled. Our culture craves attention. Unfortunately, that has been transplanted into the church. So when we get ready to go fishing we err by concentrating too much on the appearance of our fishing boat or the size of the marlin we hang on the wall. Thus our casting for fish is "on the wrong side" of the vessel.

> *We are blindly rebuilding Babel, and then we are confused when our plans for church growth implode.*

In Western culture we look for churches where we are "being fed," and bypass the ones who are truly hungry. We are blindly rebuilding Babel, and then we are confused when our plans for church growth implode. The picture of a healthy church focuses first on restored souls, not a large edifice with parking for 800 cars. Fishing for men as the Lord directs is seldom a glamorous vocation and can be smelly and dirty. God, not man, determines our reward.

Observe the spectacle of social media. We quickly discover that it's an easy substitute for intimacy and vulnerability. Facebook is no substitute for face-to-face. Face-to-face contact now includes a third "person" in the form of electronic devices. The smart phone has been so deeply integrated into our culture that it occupies a place in most conversations. Facts are checked. News items are instantaneous. Boundaries are practically nonexistent. Communication suffers from the distraction of our "smart" phone. Our priorities are acutely askew.

This is not a condemnation of technology. It's a caution flag that says distractions will prevent us from fulfilling God's highest calling on our lives. Let's be careful and get real. Many of us need to repent for allowing distractions to damage the most important relationships in our lives. Prayer is as it always has been—time set apart without distractions. Getting alone with God requires real discipline.

Imagine the sailors on a fishing trip. A gale is blowing in. Decks are awash. Marines are hauling in nets with a smartphone in one hand or with earbuds underneath hooded slickers. No one is paying attention to obvious dangers. If we fail to operate circumspectly we miss the cable on the deck, the loose boom on the mast, the wave coming over the starboard rail, the warning shout from our cohorts.

To be fishers of men, as Yeshua was teaching His disciples, exposes precarious pitfalls. In this type of environment one must be keenly aware of everything going on all around. We must keep our eyes on the prize, remembering that glory forever outshines glamour.

Nothing can ever compare with a once shackled spirit being set free.

Bigger Is Not Always Better

The result of adopting an insufficient model to advance the Kingdom is a church that places so much emphasis on the position of pastor that few pastors are capable of fulfilling their primary calling—to effectively nurture their flock. Unless a church is fortunate enough to have a pastor who has a specialized set of gifts that combines many or most of these gifts, there is little chance of building the dynamic mega-church that we blindly believe will be a success. However, this model reflects our cultural image of success, and that image won't work in church.

Since our society's corporate model of success has been transplanted into the church, the church is inappropriately measuring its success against a secular model. Thus, much of the church that claims the name of Jesus Christ does not look or act like the church the Lord intended it to be.

We applaud the achievements of those leaders who can draw a large audience and significantly impact their communities. However the primary role of a pastor is based on intimacy within the community of believers. It is for good reason that Yeshua personally disciples only twelve men. If ever there was, or will be, a person equipped for reaching the multitudes, it was Yeshua. He focused on a handful of close associates. We must do the same.

Large congregations have much to offer. It's a thing of beauty to see a big church get behind a big project. Communities are impacted. People see the benefits of organized efforts. The church itself is obviously the combination of all of its parts. When the church works effectively there is great joy in the city, and even in nations.

Recall that there are only three prescribed feasts when all men of Israel were instructed to gather on the Temple Mount to assemble as a nation. Thus the church is not called to act as a singular unit except on a few occasions during the year. These feasts correspond to Passover in spring, Shavuot in summer, and Sukkot in the fall. Did you ever wonder what Kingdom living be would like if we honored these feasts, if we did what Yeshua did, if we walked according to the model He followed?

Yeshua honored these directives from Torah. I'm not suggesting that the church has to celebrate these feasts, but I seldom even hear of our roots being acknowledged, or an understanding of the one new man, unless I'm in a church that expresses support for the movement of Messianic Judaism. All this to say, there are clear models of how Yeshua walked out His faith here on earth that we don't follow. If we call ourselves Christians, why not?

> *Yeshua focused His personal ministry on the small group with whom He walked. We couldn't ask for a better example of building a healthy, faith-based ministry.*

Yeshua focused His personal ministry on the small group with whom He walked. We couldn't ask for a better example of building a healthy, faith-based ministry. Here's the ideal model of intimate contact as we live, work, and build lasting relationships. Compact, tight, connected. That's the best way to equip.

On those occasions when Yeshua was with the multitudes, it was seldom in a traditional church setting. When it came time to meet the needs of the masses, Yeshua demonstrated His sovereignty over creation by feeding thousands at one time. Recall the episode in John 6 as a lad offers to share his personal cache of five loaves and two fishes. The Lord decides to multiply this seemingly inconsequential gift to satisfy the physical and spiritual hunger of a large number of seekers.

This scene stands in marked contrast to small, local synagogue settings. It was in these private places where the Lord could do mighty works. This is why He asked those whom He healed to keep His whereabouts discreet. Yeshua taught the masses in a boat from across the water, but when Yeshua went fishing, He asked Peter to head out to the deep. There were few witnesses and the catch was massive.

The logistics of big churches demand so much administrative capacity that the lack of personal attention becomes an inescapable casualty. Unfortunately the expanding growth of mega-churches is often at the expense of gleaning believers from smaller churches who unwittingly sacrifice intimacy to follow the herd. While the headcount swells, the migration of membership uproots parishioners from service to their local communities. Ultimately the small local church, the cornerstone of our communities, loses so many members it is unable to keep its doors open. We've seen this pattern in countless communities in Europe.

Shrinking numbers of church participants send a painful report that the message of the gospel is not being lived out with fruitfulness. And the Word of God tells us that *they will know us by our fruits* (Matthew 7:16,20). The harvest of souls is diminishing in America. This is tragic. With so much pressure on pastors to grow large churches to impact our communities, we often overlook the need for small, tightly woven groups where intimacy is established between members in nearby churches. Familiarity between leaders and laymen yields the sustained growth in churches that pleases the heart of the Father.

Corporate culture is eroding the foundation of the gospel. Instead of serving our communities, the church suffers from trying to become a community unto itself. We suffer when we mistake size and sizzle for service and sensitivity. Yeshua came to set the sinners free. Today we focus on saving the church instead of the sinners.

> *Instead of serving our communities, the church suffers from trying to become a community unto itself.*

There is much joy when a large group joins together to honor our King, but this is not the pattern of the Book of Acts. Perhaps you have noticed how the conversation for building churches inevitably designates the Book of Acts as the church model to duplicate.

The Kingdom of God suffers by not implementing the optimally effective leadership model our Lord has instructed us to use! We claim to use the Book of Acts, but don't follow its instructions. Pastors in particular, are pulled in too many directions to effectively care for their flocks. The inevitable distractions due to the details of church administration (that is too easily substituted for pastoral guidance) can dilute effective ministry and discipleship.

Too often the result is a top-heavy infrastructure delegated to fulfill the needs of the masses. As many of us work for large companies, there is a strong tendency to implement a corporate model of leadership required to manage the myriad of attributes of running a large operation. In the jumble of event-oriented activities to develop a collective culture that seems to require that the saints be entertained, inadequate attention is given to the purpose of the fivefold gifts.

Do I like to be in a big church worshipping God? Yes. It's marvelous. It's a foretaste of Heaven itself. It honors God. But there is a high price for attendance if we are not attending to the needs of our neighborhood. Churches gain identity by serving our community, not as a commodity to be bought and sold.

The Model of Moses

There was good reason for Moses' father-in-law, Jethro, to advise the leader of Israel to get much-needed assistance. Moses, as with current-day pastors, was overwhelmed with duties and deliberation. This cost Moses his peace of mind. Note in the following passage the great gift of wisdom Jethro brings to Moses. Jethro fulfilled a prophetic calling and released Moses to be a more accomplished leader. Every congregational leader requires men like Jethro, to attract *able men, such as fear God*, to form a healthy body.

> *So Moses' father-in-law said to him, "The thing that you do is not good. Both you and these people who are with you will surely wear yourselves out. For this thing is too much for you; you are not able to perform it by yourself. Listen now to my voice; I will give you counsel, and God will be with you: Stand before God for the people, so that you may bring the difficulties to God. And you shall teach them the statutes and the laws, and show them the way in which they must walk and the work they must do. Moreover you shall select from all the people able men, such as fear God, men of truth, hating covetousness; and place such over them to be rulers of thousands, rulers of hundreds, rulers of fifties, and rulers of tens. And let them judge the people at all times. Then it will be that every great matter they shall bring to you, but every small matter they themselves shall judge. So it will be easier for you, for they will bear the burden with you. If you do this thing, and God so commands you, then you will be able to endure, and all this people will also go to their place in peace"* (Exodus 18:17-23).

Churches comprised of overworked pastors and disorganized believers are ubiquitous. Pastors often feel pushed to take on administrative postures to keep things organized. Here is an excellent opportunity to seek the assistance of those with the mantle of apostle and/or prophet who possess godly wisdom to overcome the real challenges of organization.

And we must not neglect the missionary outreaches that the Lord puts on our hearts. Add to this a pastor's presumed need to instruct new believers' classes, marriage seminars, Bible studies, etc., begging the cry for assistance from those with evangelical and teaching gifts. Busyness clouds our vision for the lofty potential of our church.

How swiftly we become mired in a morass of managerial musical chairs. This would be laughable, except that this has become the norm for many congregations. This is why the Lord gave us the fivefold gifts. We recognize the need for assistance, but we fail to engage the solution designated by God.

We require insight from mature elders who hear from God. Their experiences teach us the mysteries of Messiah that have been revealed to God's holy emissaries and prophets. Ephesians 3:4-6 explains that Gentiles and Jews are co-heirs and fellow members of the same body and co-sharers of the promise in Messiah Yeshua through the Good News. A qualified elder can start a lively discussion in any study of the Word—without a pastor.

Without a Jethro to guide our pastors, the process of delegation is avoided and our overworked ministers become defensive. Common symptoms of this problem are insensitivity, withdrawal, and isolation. Our once soft-spoken leaders resort to intimidation and anger to protect frayed nerves from entanglements. Jesus needed time alone with God to discern His will. It's the same for all who wear the cloth of clergy.

In our nation the church has relinquished the majority of its assigned roles to the offices of government. The outcome of avoiding our responsibility to serve our society is that the church has allowed the civic government to try to solve problems outside of its calling. The church is called to oversee these tasks and ministries and we don't answer God's beckoning. We are ducking instead of standing tall.

We can complain about the ineffectiveness of the government until the cows come home to be milked. But the cows (our sheep) should be looking to the church to teach godly principles, not the federal government.

Structural Integrity of the Church

The nature of a shepherd's calling requires courage. But courage alone won't overcome the enemy. A major challenge we face is an internal strife that runs much deeper than church politics. This is a common cause of frustration among leaders.

Most of us dislike confrontation, so if we find ourselves under the covering of a strong-willed leader we hesitate to voice our concerns. That administrator then fails to hear the message concerning his own stubbornness or her inflexibility. Before we push back on this comment, there are reasons why we have become so defensive. Are there personality issues that manifest under pressure? We know so. But the basis for our behavioral conflicts that trigger disagreements run deep.

Let's scrutinize the structure of the church itself. We have been ignoring a foundational problem that inhibits the vitality of the church. This departure from God's blueprint is sucking the breath out of virtually every move to unify the church of believers.

Contrary to biblical guidelines, the role of pastor has been redefined in Western culture. For those pastors who are overworked, isolated, and questioning the effectiveness or purpose of their calling, there are root causes. As with the sons of Issachar (1 Chronicles 12:32), we must know the times in which we live to focus our efforts on the immediate needs of our communities. Let's identify the battle lines.

While there are innumerable causes for churches to suffer, let's direct our attention to three arenas that are mandated by God that too many churches fail to address. First is the need for unity within the Kingdom of God. Second is an understanding of freedom. Third is the need for trust. Each of these fundamental requirements are foundational to the strength of the church. While we here are concentrating on the church in Western culture, assuredly this scenario applies in broader applications that affect the health of every nation.

It is the church's responsibility to direct all three of these needs. Social programs and politics will use these terms; however, only the church can provide the moral bedrock for unity, freedom, and trust to flourish. Thomas Jefferson's Declaration of Independence rested upon an understanding that there are self-evident truths given to us by God that govern our lives and make our freedom possible:

> We hold these truths to be self-evident, that all men are created equal, that they are endowed by their Creator with certain unalienable Rights, that among these are Life, Liberty and the pursuit of Happiness.

The Need for Unity

Our nation is suffering from the lack of unity in the church. That's right, we are responsible for much of our nation's woes. Our lack of single-mindedness has encouraged the public to put our belief in God on trial. This forces the courts to judge the practicality of faith. Since faith cannot be shaped to stay within the bounds of rationality, the courts decided the Word of God is no longer deemed authoritative.

God gave us our model of freedom, not man. Freedom to worship God was the main motivating impetus for vast numbers of people to come to America. When a nation built on a godly understanding of freedom decides to redefine the foundation for that freedom, it sacrifices that which is sacred. People who are willing to die to be free built America.

It matters not if we adhere to our Constitution, if we give up on God and manufacture a differing definition of liberty. No set of rules will ever supersede God's. The Lord doesn't need to stop this. All He has to do is to allow us to have our way. It won't take long before we discover this reckless road can only lead to ruin.

Following Pentecost, unity in the Kingdom allowed the early church to spread the gospel. Unity is best described in the high priestly prayer Yeshua prayed the night before He was executed. Unity inhabits the very name of our nation. United is a state of being. When our nation takes on a foe, we call for citizens from every state, not just Missouri or Montana.

If a religion justifies taking the life of another human being simply because one has a differing belief, it lacks the love of God. Americans have always laid down their lives so freedom of religion would flourish. We know that moral superiority is impossible. It is with love, repentance, and forgiveness that God gave us His laws. That's what ultimately unites us.

The life, death, and resurrection of Yeshua is the undeniable truth of a sovereign, loving God, willing to sacrifice that which is most precious to protect and provide for His family. Any structure that is not built upon this understanding is built on sand. Any view of our Constitution that does not accept belief in God as its fundamental means of providing our values will restrict our system of justice.

We are not talking about politics. The love of God is the cornerstone of democracy, not the Democratic or Republican Party. The ability to choose is an expression of our free will. Choice is the expression of God's purposes for His creation. The state of our nation will not be united on humanistic principles.

Equality doesn't happen because we live in a free state. Equality happens because our nation and our society unequivocally accept God's guidelines for freedom. Only within the bounds of a holy, sacred, righteous standard of living can we manage to truly love and honor one another. That's what God requires of a godly nation. A system that expects the courts to judge the righteousness of God alters the relationship between God and His creation. We only get to choose whether or not we will follow His values, not change them.

A nation that is built on fear may claim to be righteous, but that is self-righteousness. Such "faith" lacks compassion. Intimidation is a powerful motivator, but it constricts those it touches and imprisons them in fear.

> *There is no fear in love. But perfect love drives out fear, because fear has to do with punishment. The one who fears is not made perfect in love* (1 John 4:18 NIV).

Fear can be used to unify, but it is not the love of God. The Lord's children are drawn together by choice, not coercion. Our desire to be members of God's Kingdom needs the unity that honors our Creator. On that Rock every nation sinks or stands.

Understanding Freedom

Freedom is the result of a righteous system of justice. Without righteousness there is no such thing as justice. Without justice there is no such thing as freedom. Our laws are laid on a biblical foundation. It is a biblical code of ethics that makes our freedom possible. Without a common understanding of justice we will never be united. And unless we are united under a workable judicial and legislative system that recognizes its own foundation, freedom will become illusive, subjective, and impossible to ascertain.

> *Without a common understanding of justice we will never be united.*

No matter how equitable we try to make our laws, it is impossible to create a just society without a biblical foundation. The finest example of this is the 40-year reign of King Solomon over Israel. Clearly he had God's favor. No empire will stand the test of time unless it is built on God's everlasting laws.

The United States of America is founded on godly principles. If our culture chooses to exaggerate the meaning of freedom to include and embrace immorality, we overstretch the fabric of our sails to the degree where the wind of the Holy Spirit, which is meant to power our vessel, passes through torn canvas. We will become a people who celebrate lifestyle, at the cost of our character. We must stand against sacrificing any freedom, unless that so-called "freedom" proves to be counterfeit.

> *Having a form of godliness but denying its power. And from such people turn away!* (2 Timothy 3:5)

A nation without rock-solid spiritual underpinnings will disintegrate. Trying to save the union, President Abraham Lincoln quoted the Holy Scriptures, "a house divided against itself cannot stand." I'm reminded of Samson, who having lost his sight, presses on the pillars of the Philistine temple. As that shrine of false religion collapses, he lays down his own life in the ultimate sacrificial gesture to prevent his immoral foes from overrunning his native land (Judges 19).

Instead of leading our citizens in righteousness, according to our Lord's model, the United States of America considers redefining our freedoms in terms of a so-called "separation" of church and state. This "newly discovered" destructive idea (which somehow eluded our nation's leaders for well over two centuries), has swollen into a rallying cry that was never the intent of our founders. It flies in the face of a country that built a foundation of freedoms endowed by our Creator. It's God, not man, who instructed us how to honor one another in the act of creation. Such division over the definition of "separation" invites God's intervention.

This perception of a freedom that requires acceptance of morally disobedient behavior can only take root if the church is made to appear as if it restricts our liberties. Additionally, this type of thinking has to ignore the immeasurable benefits the Kingdom of God has brought to humanity. How is that possible? Such a worldview is the result of a steep moral decline both within and without the church.

The world can't undermine God's design for His Kingdom. But a church so disempowered by its own lack of cohesiveness may lack the required resolve and essential unity to squash such an immoral backlash. The world, by turning against the church, blames the One True God who gave us our freedom for not giving us enough.

This type of religious persecution wants to turn the tables on a nation that was created out of the need to express our right to worship God into a country that insists that there must be more (or less) to this life that what God offers. This also means the leadership of a church that won't fight this heresy with every last ounce of strength must have determined there is something the world offers that is more attractive than what our God can supply. Hogwash.

The Kingdom of God is the most liberating environment ever conceived. No one would ever want to sacrifice this freedom unless they have been led to believe there was something better. Perhaps this is the result of living in an insulated nation that offers so many creature comforts that walking in the Spirit seems to have lost its luster.

Nevertheless, the church throughout history has faced every conceivable obstacle and flourished, so it's only a matter of time before the foibles of man's ways will wither away and we return with repentant hearts to the One who truly loves us.

The Spirit of America was called forth by the first to come here. This Spirit has been intentionally reaffirmed by every wave of immigration for centuries. The great majority of these newcomers specifically identified God as sovereign over America. The only "separation" mentioned (which is never stated in the Declaration of Independence, the Constitution, the Bill of Rights or any amendments) was to prevent the state from endorsing or imposing any specific sect or denomination from defining our faith. The designation for the Spirit of America has always been to prevent the state from dictating to the church. If our state continues to enforce its sovereignty over God's sovereignty—our nation will suffer immensely.

We don't know what this will look like. Perhaps economic fallout or current signs of weather instability are indeed instigated by man. But the cause for correction would be due to our spiritual bankruptcy, not national debt or climate change from burning fossil fuels. When our relationship with God is restored, so shall it be with the United States of America. Old glory is dependent upon God's glory. That's the banner that must be held high for the Spirit of America to prevail.

I don't want to start a debate about morality. I want my fellow patriots to consider who God is. I don't believe it will satisfy anyone's goals to try to redefine God, to mold Him into an image that is acceptable to us by insisting that He is very different from whom He has revealed Himself to be. The fact is we have been made to reflect His image. Thus our goal is to be like Him. That includes every aspect of life. Thus we will hold on to God's standards proclaimed in John 8:32 (NIV): *"Then you will know the truth, and the truth will set you free."*

Why does this verse begin with *"Then"*? It's because the preceding verse, John 8:31, gives us the condition for knowing the truth. That is, *"To the Jews who had believed him, Jesus said, 'If you hold to my teaching, you are really my disciples.'"* Two things become readily apparent. First, Jesus is speaking to people who believe; and second, truth will be revealed to those who *"hold to my teaching...."* Let's think on that. Knowing the truth and being set free by this truth is conditional upon believing in Yeshua and following His precepts. Everyone quotes verse 32, but we fail to know its context.

Truth is not relative. Truth is based on our relationship with God. Learn from this!

Trust in God

Our forefathers never intended to reduce the church's influence on the state. However, they did intend to reduce the state's influence over the church. Please note that we decided to "reduce," not eliminate. From the beginning, by design, there is to be a cooperative association between the state and the church, just as there is between the state and any charitable organization. The church is God's banner of protection over the state that supports its existence. Our nation is designed as a mutualistic symbiotic relationship between church and state—both institutions depend upon, and benefit from, one another.

Our United States protects groups with charitable causes. It sees them as beneficial to society and grants them tax-free status because they perform tasks that improve our quality of life. This is especially true for the faith-based community, as Judeo-Christian principles were employed to establish law and order. Without these values we damage our quality of life. Government without faith-based influence is a ship without a rudder.

Prayer before meetings and worship of God acknowledge our need for divine providence. These represent our dependence on a Savior. They are not expressions of religion and our government is not telling us how we are to honor God. Religion is a teaching of a specific set of activities for expressing our faith. We can make room for new, mutually beneficial ideas without denigrating our spiritual heritage.

In recent days this essential function of maintaining a working, balanced relationship between church and state has been seriously contested. Historically, there have often been social implications for the law; however, the standing of the church as the moral compass has never been so severely diminished.

Because America has attracted so many cultures, there will always be an effort to be inclusive for newcomers—freedom makes the USA quite appealing. Let us never forget that the environment of freedom will bring us the fresh air we desire as long as we allow the wind of the Holy Spirit to blow free. This is the Spirit of America that the pilgrims and the pioneers sought. They came here looking for a place where they could worship God without governmental persecution.

Yielding to spiritual forces that release, rather than repress, comes from honoring God and yielding to Him and to Him alone. The government does not dictate to religions; however, the government does recognize the God we serve has blessed our nation abundantly because we protect human life and dignity. Thus we prominently print on all our currency the truth that gives our nation its foundation, "In God We Trust." Pray that we never stray from this core belief.

Such values are not man-made. So as man attempts to bring a value system of his own making—one that diminishes life—even if mankind claims it is of God, it will not stand the test of the sanctity of life. Life is given to us. It is a gift of a loving God. Therefore every act of humanity must be scrutinized and weighed with lovingkindness, mercy, and forgiveness to honor God's gift to us of freedom.

Thankfully God's Word gives us a blueprint to determine the feasibility of our decisions. Using the Bible and biblical principles is not violating the separation of church and state. Conversely, dictating how an individual should or shouldn't worship God in the United States of America is a violation of that principle.

Ever the more so, if an individual is punished for not worshipping God, or one claiming to be a prophet, in a particular fashion we have stepped over the boundaries for building a free nation. Forcing faith is un-American and ungodly. This type of religion will not hold root on our soil.

Trust in God is a biblical principle. America will not stand as a nation if she fails to trust in God. If the public decides that it wishes to place its trust in any other entity, it has the right to do so. But know that the moment this happens, the divinely ordained Spirit of America suffers. God Almighty, not our government, has given us the power to decide for our nation to increase or cease. There are many groups, even nations that would like to destroy us. Our future is not predetermined. For us to survive is for us to trust in God.

Our divided and diminished church is becoming too diluted to effectively influence our culture. As evil forces inject their poisons into the world, we hear some objections, but there is no collective church to condemn their behavior. A passive church morality risks being redefined to emphasize permissiveness to be the highest order of expressing one's identity, all in the name of freedom. We lift up tolerance as the church hesitates to speak out against those who disagree with us, because we feel obligated to allow others to exercise their "freedoms." This is weak-kneed faith. This passivity pumps up the pride of our persecutors.

We tend to overlook the fact that many of these other communities have no desire to return the favor of forgiveness—a foundational biblical principle. In fact, they are outspokenly anti-American, anti-Semitic, and anti-Christian. They mean to destroy those who naively expect them to give homage to Americans and their fellow human beings because we won't call out their sin. Yes, we are to forgive; but we are not to condone behavior that justifies sin in the name of freedom.

Freedom is being redefined as permissiveness; even if that permissiveness leads to our own destruction. The idealism that drives this flawed thinking has turned against itself and is consuming its host. If we are unable to reverse this tide we will have only ourselves to blame. America is the land of liberty within the framework that honors the sanctity of righteous living. That's how God makes us free.

Because we have allowed evil to triumph and sin to be accepted in our high places, a shift will come. As our nation vocally lauds unbridled permissiveness, we grieve the heart of God. He will move His hand. The church must identify an error, but we are not supposed to judge. We demonstrate forgiveness, which encourages the sinner to make a better choice. The rallying cry for righteousness and a hand of mercy unites us and makes us one. That's how we mend our broken nets.

Chapter 14

The Fivefold Ministry

Unity of the Spirit

Why would the apostle Paul situate his teaching about the responsibility of leaders in the city of Ephesus? Ephesus was once a thriving port with a broad sphere of influence around the world. During that era, conflicting interpretations on spiritual matters interfered with the growth of the early church. This resulted in a multiplicity of religious theories being expounded upon a naïve and unsuspecting populace comprised from a variety of cultures. Theological debate inevitably unearthed division and confusion.

Ephesus looked much like our contemporary world. Diverse doctrines. Cross-cultural customs. Various values. To fish in these waters required genuine, godly wisdom, if you will, a heavenly perspective. From the opening statements in this epistle, Paul takes us to the lofty heights of heavenly places. He steps out by explaining our standing before a Holy God, who loves us enough to make us holy and blameless. Paul assures us that we have been purposely put here to fulfill God's will. What's more, the apostle reveals God's plan for all humanity and the ultimate unifying of Jews and Gentiles.

Once this stage has been set, The Lord uses Paul to explain how these ministerial callings of apostle, prophet, evangelist, pastor, and teacher should be used to develop a strong, mature, unified body. These five types of leaders reflect the avenues God chooses to educate and prepare believers to build His Kingdom.

Under divine inspiration to release believers to achieve their highest calling, Paul reveals God's solution for walking in unity—that believers in Messiah Yeshua would *"walk worthy of the calling with which you were called"* (Ephesians 4:1). The City of Ephesus became the bedrock Paul would use to present God's grand design that His followers unite as one new man.

One might wonder how our calling could affect unity. Paul explains to the disciples of Yeshua that we must exemplify love by adopting the attributes of humility. True humility shows up as loving service to those in need. Fulfilling our calling to humbly serve those in need brings the family of believers into harmony. Paul advises, *"endeavoring to keep the unity of the Spirit in the bond of peace"* (Ephesians 4:3).

The church cannot exhibit this bond of peace without unity of the Spirit. And unity of the Spirit cannot be accomplished within the Kingdom of God unless we follow the model given to us by God. To accomplish His goals, the Lord appoints the fivefold leadership gifts to guide His body, of which *He Himself* is the Head, how to move in unison to demonstrate lovingkindness. To be unified, the body must follow the Head. This lesson is vital—we must not overlook the essential reasons why Yeshua, the Head of the body of believers, dispensed leadership into these key callings.

Although these five roles appear on the surface to be simple to discern, they are seldom employed in contemporary ministry. We have not adhered to the Lord's directive. This leaves His church highly vulnerable to leadership models that fail to meet our King's design for His Kingdom. When we do follow Yeshua, everything falls into place in perfect harmony. The fruit of the Spirit prevails and the Kingdom of God is at hand!

> *The king's heart is in the hand of the Lord, like the rivers of water; He turns it wherever He wishes* (Proverbs 21:1).

Life Forevermore

The Lord's designated purpose for the fivefold offices is to teach and equip. This is how Jesus instructs us to extend the Kingdom of God. We are predestined to do the good works that God has established. This is not employing a special formula for success. It's God's way of showing us that He promises to bless us for following—for being obedient to His ways. Psalm 133 confirms His blessing for unity.

> *Behold, how good and how pleasant it is for brethren to* ***dwell together in unity!*** *It is like the precious oil upon the head, running down on the beard, the beard of Aaron, running down on the edge of his garments. It is like the dew of Hermon, descending upon the mountains of Zion. For there the Lord commanded the blessing—* ***life forevermore.***

This Scripture passage is a showstopper. The Lord commands a blessing to fall upon His children when we *dwell together in unity!* I don't know about you, but when God gives a commandment, it's His highest order of building covenant. He will not break His word to us. He promises to do His part; likewise, we must do ours.

And what is the promise that God makes? *Life forevermore.* I won't even try to download that one. Only God can make such a promise. It doesn't get better than this.

As our Lord sent the disciples out two by two, He was teaching us His method of building *both* the church and its future leaders as we impact our local communities with the gospel. We need to see the Holy Spirit in action. We need to see the Lord meet us at our point of penetration into the world. We need to experience God with us in the mission field. This is an irresistible witness to our world. And the world will see that God's promises are true.

Church leadership and discipleship are crucial. Building church attendance and constructing larger sanctuaries are *not* biblical mandates.

Yet, look where we focus the majority of our energy: membership, giving, programs, building funds. Yes, these functions are important, but they are means to a much greater end. God is concerned about the depth of our character, not the height of our steeple.

> *God is concerned about the depth of our character, not the height of our steeple.*

An attractive edifice may make church members feel good, but it ignores the biblical instruction to place those in need above even our own needs. A better-looking fishing boat doesn't catch more fish. The best catch comes from a well-trained, unified crew who works together toward a common goal—nets full of fish hungry for eternity with Jesus.

Hand in Glove

I'd like to use a simple illustration that I've heard to explain the roles of the offices in a user-friendly fashion. We can call this a "warm handshake."

As the digits on a hand, consider their appropriate applications. The thumb represents an apostle. In its opposing position from the other fingers, we are able to grasp and manipulate objects. This allows us to use tools and gives us leverage to do great works. Apostles plant churches and ministries. They are the visionaries of the church.

The first finger is used for pointing. This is the calling of the prophet. He or she directs and focuses our attention to the matter at hand. A prophet is someone who can discern God's vision for an individual, family, church, community, region, and even for nations. In the contemporary church, a prophet is called to build up, to edify so that the body of believers would understand their lofty calling to serve.

The center finger has the greatest reach. Evangelism is the pinnacle of ministry. As Yeshua came to save those who are lost, this office is itinerant and often goes to great lengths to spread the Word of God. Those gifted with this calling often find themselves in the far corners of the planet. They are the ultimate missionaries and are most adept at casting out and hauling in the nets filled with fresh fish.

The fourth, or ring finger, represents committed relationships. The pastor is called to intimacy with the flock. These are the shepherds who best know the issues of their parishioners. They are on hand for the highs and lows of each person's life. They can best minister to the problems and solutions their members face. They are in the hospitals and on the frontlines. Commitment is the bedrock of intimacy.

The little finger completes the picture. The doctrines and details of our faith define the whole counsel of God. Such intricacies bring a depth of understanding of the nature of our God and His purpose for our lives. Solid teaching strengthens the walk of every believer. Yeshua was able to demonstrate the way for us to walk out our faith by teaching parables—simple illustrations that exemplify principles and practices.

These five digits, properly working in unison, form the whole hand and can lead the symphony of believers to do the works that God has called us to perform:

> *to equip his people for works of service, so that the body of Christ may be built up until we all reach unity in the faith and in the knowledge of the Son of God and become mature, attaining to the whole measure of the fullness of Christ* (Ephesians 4:12-13 NIV).

The Offices

When the five offices of apostle, prophet, evangelist, pastor, and teacher are operating with proper understanding of their calling, the church is united, effective, and capable of dynamic power and outreach. The Lord gave us this structure so we would employ it.

Today there are tens of thousands of different groupings of believers. The lack of unity signifies the diluted ability to solve significant challenges to advance His Kingdom. In our nation the church has relinquished the majority of its assigned roles to the offices of government. The outcome of avoiding our responsibility to serve our society is that the church has allowed the civic government to try to solve problems outside of its calling.

"…it's what we know that ain't so."

I am reminded of a Will Rogers quotation, "It isn't what we don't know that gives us trouble, it's what we know that ain't so."

The church knows what it's called to do. The problem is that we shirk our responsibilities. The church has pulled back from operating as a proactive partner in overcoming difficulties. With this diminished role, too little is accomplished and problems are swept under the rug. As a result, poverty, hunger, sickness, slavery, and violence continue to plague our world. Of course I'm not saying that all of these difficulties would disappear, just that we would be able to address them with far greater positive results.

Without the church's active, focused efforts to tackle society's ills, we try the humanist approach of relegating our headaches to governments that, despite their best intentions to improve our plight, fall short. In fact, there is ample evidence that many of our worst situations are perpetuated and exacerbated by the failed policies and the shortsightedness foisted upon an ill-informed public by governing bodies.

The church allows its callings and responsibilities to be misappropriated. Thus, the church is misaligned. Western culture has so influenced the church in North America, that we have reordered God's design for how to function in ministry. It won't work. Add to that our misplaced desires to dump our problems on others, avoiding the high calling on believers to embrace our destiny as God's designated vessels eager to face these challenges.

But there is Good News. When we do what the Lord has called us to do, He will bless us. He will bless His church. God hasn't stopped loving His church. He is just waiting for us to do what He has called us to do. As leaders in the church come to realize the necessity for service to our communities, the manifest blessings of Heaven will bring the harvest we all long to see. The tools to accomplish this goal have been laid out in the Holy Scriptures.

When Paul spoke to the Ephesians, he showed them the immeasurable heights God wants us to experience by employing His grand design.

These fivefold gifts have distinct, complementary callings. Once we grasp the purpose for these leadership ministries, the body of believers will be better suited to do the equipping that our Lord has assigned us. Ironically, most of us understand, and can even describe these callings. Yet the church fails to exercise and practice the purposes for these ministries.

Under the New Covenant, due to the coming of our King and the canonization of the Holy Scriptures, our roles have been redefined. Again, this will not be news to most of us. The challenge we face today is in the implementation of what God has already ordained. The future of the church will be determined by our ability to adjust to God's high calling as we respond to our world's needs—His way.

> *"For My thoughts are not your thoughts, nor are your ways My ways," says the Lord. "For as the heavens are higher than the earth, so are My ways higher than your ways, and My thoughts than your thoughts"* (Isaiah 55:8-9).

Leadership Calls

The following is a brief overview of the roles of authority for church government.

Apostle: A mature leader with visionary gifts and capabilities. Apostles plant churches and oversee their early development.

Often they administer a number of churches with similar callings, ministries, and geographical consistencies. They interpret church doctrines. Peter and Paul are the classic examples.

Prophet: One who edifies and encourages the saints. Often a prophet will discern truths and underlying causes for circumstances. They point out gifting and calling over individuals, ministries, and geographical regions. Prophets often pair up with apostles (Moses and Aaron) to give spiritual insight and direction for the body.

Evangelist: A person who shares the vision for God's gift of salvation; great fishers of men. These are itinerant individuals whose ministries sometimes carry them around the globe. They have zeal to preach the gospel and plant the seeds of revival. This is the easiest office to identify, as its role hasn't been reinterpreted.

Pastor: A leader with the gift of ministering to the saints. Here is where the ministry of the gospel becomes personal and the application of the Word gets connected to life events. As affiliated with shepherds, this office requires a closeness and intimacy with the members of the flock.

Teacher: A wise theologian who knows how to apply spiritual principles to life. One who grasps the messages of the gospel and faithfully applies and exemplifies God's parables to life's circumstances by communicating these principles to others.

It is not my intention to unpack all of the theological issues regarding these five offices. I'll leave that to the apologists. It is essential that we become aware of ways that we address these different offices in both healthy and unhealthy ways. In the West we have a tendency to apply culturally relevant models to the church that reflect corporate value systems, but are biblically inconsistent. The result is a church that suffers ridicule, because it doesn't effectively catch and release disciples.

> *For the earnest expectation of the creation eagerly waits for the revealing of the sons of God* (Romans 8:19).

Challenges and Snares

The following are some significant obstacles that our leaders often face.

Apostle: Often a self-appointed leader with a strong desire to lead and teach the Word of God. An apostle needs accountability, as do all leaders in every position. Apostles can see where the Lord is calling His body to minister and plant new churches, but can get spread too thin by administrative details. It is not unusual to see pastors inadvertently taking on this role, contrary to their calling.

Prophet: Claiming this office is like painting a target on your chest. The body is quick to embrace or disgrace any who use this title. Instead of being able to offer sound wisdom to the apostles and other leaders in the body, a prophet spends too much time defending his or her calling. Prophets are placed here on earth to assist us in discerning the calling and moves of God. This position has been under attack.

While many prophets may have gifts of discernment, the role is not merely to act as a fortuneteller for saints who want to discover who their spouse is going to be or where our kids should go to college. Prophets are needed to direct the battle against the forces of darkness.

Evangelists: Such who fulfill this calling are gifted communicators. They know how to share the gospel, and often will go to great lengths to lead souls to our King. Of all the offices listed, contemporary evangelists remain closest to his or her intended call.

Pastors: As the church has adopted more and more of Western culture, the role of pastor has shifted to resemble CEO. Such administrative activities are not essential for many pastors, especially those who associate with mature advisers. Pastors often take too much on their plate. Church planting, ministry, teaching, and counseling combine to take on way too much weight and responsibility. This usually occurs by default, as the other offices are not being filled or properly adhered to.

Teachers: Teachers need to share gospel principles with more than our youth. The challenge here is that teachers seldom are given the opportunity. We relegate teachers to the primary role of taking care of young believers and miss the depth of knowledge they are called to disseminate to the entire body of Messiah. Being a pastor often requires teaching, but we also need to hear from others who can school us on how to divide the Word.

Needless to say, the real challenge to implement these offices comes as we see how many leaders have the maturity to lay down their crowns and allow their peers to recognize the gifts and the callings so these offices can be filled. The church needs to learn how to accept each mantle sovereignly given to them by the Lord and appoint those worthy to fill these roles. As we act according to each of our individual callings, the church will flourish.

Part IV

Walking on Water

Chapter 15

The Tipping Point

Acts chapter 6 presents an unexpected, and often overlooked blueprint for nothing less than the Great Awakening of the church in the first century. I liken this relatively obscure portion of the Book of Acts to the fulcrum on a seesaw. It is here, at the center of the teeter-totter, where one finds the tipping point. This is the spot where the Lord reveals His destiny for His loyal followers—the fishers of men.

Invariably the sense of overcoming gravity with such minimal effort brings whoops and hollers from every child. In my own youth my father constructed a seesaw that rotated in the middle, allowing us to swivel round in circles as we careened up and down hovering above the ground. We wore a circle through the lawn where our feet shoved off the earth. Delightful.

With a seesaw, the most obvious activity occurs at either end. Here one sits upon a painted plank opposite a chosen friend enjoying the greatly exaggerated upward and downward motion, even requiring a handle to maintain a firm grip. Yet, it is the midpoint where balance and harmony find firm footing.

This leverage at the fulcrum permits great burdens to be lifted. Of course our eyes are drawn to the swings from low to high and back again. And our ears are filled with joyful screams as kids "lose their lunch" at the apex.

All this is made possible by the fulcrum. All the commotion at the extremes is scarcely detectable in the middle. Yet that seemingly slight shift at the tipping point is nothing less than catalytic to the Kingdom. God uses this dynamic point of leverage in Acts 6 to launch His Holy Spirit—to spur us on to do the good works for which He has prepared us. This witness of God's Majestic Glory inspires all who hope in Him.

Remember that sense of weightlessness as the teeter-totter reaches its utmost elevation? This is similar to what Peter felt as he walked on the water. Our spirits rise when we partner together with fellow members of the household of faith. Let's magnify that elation as the body of believers comes together as one new man and the Lord tips His scales of justice to bring His next Great Awakening to our soil.

A Light to the Gentiles

For the sake of this example of the tipping point, I'm going to use Acts 1 and 2 and Acts 9 and 10 as opposite ends of the teeter-totter. Acts chapter 6 will represent the center point.

Following Jesus' ascension to Heaven, the second chapter of Acts depicts Pentecost, which we correlate to the near side of our seesaw. We see awesome manifestations of the Spirit of God moving in the supernatural realm among the followers of Yeshua. What a picture of the outpouring of the Holy Spirit. Tongues of fire! Deliverance from demons! Thousands coming to faith day after day!

We often hear preachers calling out for a move of the Spirit reminiscent of Acts 2. We catch their sermonic pleas reverberating from the rafters, "Oh that we would return to those golden days when God moved so overtly!" We long for such an obvious and undeniable witness of God's power. To carry our analogy, this display of God's glory marks the push-off point for one end of the seesaw to rise.

On the far end of the seesaw we find Acts 9 and 10. In chapter 9, Saul runs into a spiritual brick wall that literally prevents him from continuing to exist without assistance. Following that dramatic Road to Damascus conversion, we experience the story of Peter, divinely called to visit Cornelius' residence. In both instances these patriarchs run smack dab into a different game plan. Both presume to know how to walk out his faith. *Elohim* intervenes with supernatural encounters that permanently alter their view of themselves, their life courses, and their perception of God Almighty.

Delving deeper in Acts 10, according to their religious dictates, Jews were not allowed to set foot inside a Roman household. But the Lord is up to doing something dramatic that will redirect the course of history. Lo and behold, Peter's testimony of Yeshua going to Cornelius' family results in the Holy Spirit being poured out on the Gentiles! And we know Paul's apostolic avenue will couple both people groups as well. The Kingdom of God had entered a new era. Other nations are being drawn into a Spirit-filled relationship with God, in tandem with Israel. God's chosen family is growing—rapidly.

This signifies an undeniable exposition of God at work in the midst of us. With Cornelius' confession of faith, the other side of the teeter-totter has been pushed into motion. The two ends—one for Jews and the other for Gentiles—now commence a steady cycle of cooperative ministry to bless both people groups. As each participant rises to new heights, the other prepares to push off the ground. Now, by using the counterweight provided by the previously estranged partner on the opposite end, each assists the other in a mutually beneficial lift toward Heaven.

What a picture of symmetry—Jews and Gentiles harmoniously propelling one another to new heights, fulfilling Isaiah's prophecy:

> *Thus says God the Lord, who created the heavens and stretched them out, who spread forth the earth and that which comes from it, who gives breath to the people on it, and spirit to those who walk on it: "I, the Lord, have called You in righteousness, and will hold Your hand; I will keep You and give You as a covenant to the people,*

> ***as a light to the Gentiles*** *to open blind eyes, to bring out prisoners from the prison, those who sit in darkness from the prison house. I am the Lord, that is My name; and My glory I will not give to another, nor My praise to carved images. Behold, the former things have come to pass, and new things I declare; before they spring forth I tell you of them"* (Isaiah 42:5-9).

Because the enmity, the striving between Jews and Gentiles, was eliminated by the atoning sacrifice of Yeshua, the descendants of Israel and the peoples of the nations can now live as one. Current events on the political stage overlook the sovereign plans of God. Our Lord's promise to Israel is being fulfilled, and the rejection of the world will not stand in the way of His ultimate purposes for this small nation. God made His covenant with Israel. His covenant is unbreakable.

An exceptional example of communities reaching out to each other with mutual respect is the *Navajo-Israel Agricultural Gathering*, a cooperative team effort to bring experts from Israel to partner with Native American farmers to turn their deserts into gardens. For more information on this extraordinary team effort, please see Noteworthy Ketches in the back of the book.

Just as Goliath mocked David, Israel will suffer rejection and humiliation, but she will overcome every plan of the enemy because God's purposes must be fulfilled. It is divinely predestined that God will use Israel to demonstrate His righteousness. Furthermore, it is God's promise to accept all who come to believe that Yeshua is the Son of God, be they Jew or Gentile. The world may renounce Israel, but Yahweh is the God of Israel (Exodus 3:15; 5:1; 24:10; 32:27, 34:23). He stands secure and He will never remove His hand from this nation.

God brings all nations together under the banner of His Son. The only thing preventing us from seeing and receiving His grand design is our own pride. He has destined humanity to be one new man. This is, was, and will always be the Lord's doing. This is not possible according to man's plans—this identity requires a supernatural outpouring of God's Spirit. Ultimately, just like Goliath, the giant of division has toppled, as we fulfill Jesus' prayer to be one in Him.

Some may complain that it hasn't happened the way they thought it was supposed to. Others may object to God having a Son. Perhaps the idea of torture and rejection of Jesus seems implacable. Was taking a curse on His being the only way for Yeshua to save humankind? How will Jews illuminate Gentiles? These theological questions, and more like these, will be debated until the soon Second Coming.

More than anything, we must be grateful that our God loves us, is good, and merciful.

God's ways are not our ways. We are His creation, and although He has given us great gifts, it is up to Him to determine the ways, the times, and the ultimate purpose for everything under His watchful, ever-caring eyes. More than anything, we must be grateful that our God loves us, is good, and merciful.

Israel—the Big Fish

The impact of Yeshua's entry into the world of humanity was so profound that, to honor God's sovereignty, we reset our calendars to the very hour in which He sent His Son. Time not only stopped, it was redefined. The Ancient of Days gave us His Word, and it became flesh and He, Yeshua, the Messiah of Israel, dwelled among us. His Word will outlast every life. Time itself was established to allow us a lens through which we can see God's sovereign hand at work.

Centuries have passed. Church history and the return of the Jews to their homeland have led us to this season. And the Word of God is manifest. God decided to use the separation of powers within the surviving first century Jewish leadership to confound Israel. The very ones who insisted that Rome sentence Yeshua to the cursed death on the cross will be the same religious authorities who, one day, will praise, honor, and magnify His matchless name—Yeshua HaMashiach, Jesus the Messiah.

At Pentecost, many Israeli Jews came to faith in Yeshua, but others resisted. Since those days, the gospel has spread across land and sea. Nowadays, the majority of Abraham's descendants continue to reject their Jewish Messiah—despite the fact that their neighbors on other continents have accepted Him and spread His Good News. Only an omniscient God could conceive and orchestrate such a Master's Plan for the salvation of humanity. Only a God in Heaven has a vision for relationships that transcend time.

Israel now stands more and more isolated from the very nations she has honored by protecting God's Word and blessing our world. About 1.8 billion Gentile souls profess Yeshua as Lord. 18 million people call themselves Jews. Of these Jews, less than 1 percent identifies Yeshua as Messiah. For every Jewish person who looks to Israel as home, there are a thousand believing Gentiles. And for every Jewish person who has come to faith in Yeshua, there are 99 who still look elsewhere. In short, for every Jewish person who professes Yeshua is who He says He is, the Messiah of Israel, there are 10,000 believing Gentiles. Yet the call to be a light to the Gentiles is being illuminated by this handful of believing Jews who stand on God's Word!

This partnership with Jew and Gentile, which Paul expresses in Romans chapters 9 through 11, is the culmination of God's Kingdom here on the earth. This is the book that Paul wrote to Rome. Unlike all of his other epistles written to the different churches that probably had some Jewish membership in divinely appointed outposts in other nations, Paul wrote this one to Rome—the political, economic, and military power center of the world.

And what did Paul have to say to the power brokers of his day? He gave them the gospel and told them that those of Gentile heritage would be joined to those of Jewish ancestry, as both groups were branches to be grafted into the same olive tree that represented Israel!

And there the answer has been, right under our noses for thousands of years. It is no accident that both of the most obvious acts of God's intervention into the affairs of humanity happened at the Passover. First the release of Israel from captivity, and second, the coming of the Promised One out of King David's lineage. As Jews have recited for millennia during their annual Passover Feast:

> *The stone which the builders rejected has become the chief cornerstone. This was the Lord's doing; It is marvelous in our eyes. This is the day the Lord has made; we will rejoice and be glad in it* (Psalm 118:22-24).

The Lord's intentional separation of Jews from other nations, as set into motion in the Old Testament, has now been superseded. That preliminary season has been completed. Humanity has come under a New Covenant. Yeshua is the Rejected Stone that is the Chief Cornerstone. There is no better testimony of this phenomenon than the Book of Ephesians' description of Jew and Gentile reconciled as one new man through Christ:

> *Therefore remember that you, once Gentiles in the flesh— who are called Uncircumcision by what is called the Circumcision made in the flesh by hands— that at that time you were without Christ, being aliens from the commonwealth of Israel and strangers from the covenants of promise, having no hope and without God in the world. But now in Christ Jesus you who once were far off have been brought near by the blood of Christ.*
>
> *For He Himself is our peace, who has made both one, and has broken down the middle wall of separation, having abolished in His flesh the enmity, that is, the law of commandments contained in ordinances, so as to create in Himself* **one new man** *from the two, thus making peace, and that He might reconcile them both to God in one body through the cross, thereby putting to death the enmity. And He came and preached peace to you who were afar off and*

to those who were near. For through Him we both have access by one Spirit to the Father.

Now, therefore, you are no longer strangers and foreigners, but fellow citizens with the saints and members of the household of God, having been built on the foundation of the apostles and prophets, Jesus Christ Himself being the chief cornerstone, in whom the whole building, being fitted together, grows into a holy temple in the Lord, in whom you also are being built together for a dwelling place of God in the Spirit (Ephesians 2:11-22).

It is within this light of reconciliation that we need to take a fresh look at the relationship between Jews and Gentiles in our contemporary world. There is a grand design for humanity that God has orchestrated in our midst and most of humanity, even including the very church that comprises the body of believers, is tragically unaware. For too long, too much of the church, that institution ordained by God to carry the Good News of salvation to the Jews and to the nations, has been distracted and misled. Enough already.

> *Our efforts to capture Israel are as futile as Peter's attempts to fish without the favor of Yeshua.*

We are specifically told that the behavior of believers will lead Israel to jealousy. This is how we are to fish for the Jews—through demonstrations of love. Yet we watch the world and its governing organizations battle against the existence of that narrow strip of turf. Our efforts to capture Israel are as futile as Peter's attempts to fish without the favor of Yeshua. When He appears and tells us to let down our nets on the other side of the boat, it's a whole new world for the Jews.

A simple, effective, God-ordained model of mobilizing the church was given to us in Acts 6. By the time Paul writes to those in Ephesus, we hear his burning desire to lift our eyes to the Majestic

Glory, the domain of the heavenly hosts, and see our Father's grand design for unity. Those willing to submit to this calling have changed the course of human history.

During the first century, the Jews and Gentiles who responded to God's calling, joined as one new man. This resulted in an unprecedented release of the gospel, as Yeshua's message of love exploded around the earth. Sadly, the church has taken close to 2,000 years to rediscover and dynamically apply this missive.

In an unprecedented outreach, *Kehilat HaCarmel* sits atop Mount Carmel where both Arab Christians and Messianic Jews stand together as one worshipping Yeshua as the Messiah of Israel. More information about this amazing community of believers can be found in the Noteworthy Ketches section in the back of the book.

Of course there have been notable times of awakening and revival, but the coming move of God will supplant everything that has come before. Unfortunately, there will also be a corresponding season of persecution, as our enemy will do everything he can to dissuade and persuade the world that God is nonexistent, and that Jesus is not whom He said He is. There is a real evil that exists, and the one behind it means to do all he can to imprison humanity through fear, intimidation, and death. Satan started in the Garden of Eden and he hasn't changed his schemes. He does not want to see us loving God or each other.

It is not hard to see the difference between good and evil. Clearly, the face of our foe only knows control. Genuine love and forgiveness and an appreciation for the value of every human life are the measuring scales for testing every scheme. If there is no forgiveness, you are not looking at our God.

So I invite you to "grab a partner," jump on board the teeter-totter and discover the fulfilling life of harmony within the Kingdom of God, where both Jews and Gentiles worship the same Lord and Savior. The choice is yours. I urge you to grab hold of your nets. Israel is the Big Fish.

Chapter 16

Selecting the Seven

Step by Step

The beginning of Acts chapter 6 recounts the history of choosing and releasing seven deacons. This landmark event reveals a prescribed pattern of selection that our contemporary church needs to scrutinize. Let's review.

> *Now in those days, when the number of the disciples was multiplying, there arose a complaint against the Hebrews by the Hellenists, because their widows were neglected in the daily distribution. Then the twelve summoned the multitude of the disciples and said, "It is not desirable that we should leave the word of God and serve tables. Therefore, brethren,* **seek out from among you seven men of good reputation, full of the Holy Spirit and wisdom**, *whom we may appoint over this business; but we will give ourselves continually to prayer and to the ministry of the word." And the saying pleased the whole multitude. And they chose Stephen, a man full of faith and the Holy Spirit, and Philip, Prochorus, Nicanor, Timon, Parmenas, and Nicolas, a proselyte from Antioch, whom they set before the apostles; and when they had prayed, they laid hands on them. Then* **the word of God spread***, and the* **number**

of the disciples multiplied greatly *in Jerusalem, and a great many of the priests were obedient to the faith* (Acts 6:1-7).

These first seven verses regarding these seven saints correspond to seven significant steps:

1. A difficult situation is recognized within the community of believers and a complaint is filed with their leaders: widows are being neglected in the daily distribution.
2. The apostles recognize their need to address the issue, yet realize they cannot neglect their own calling to study the Word, nor do they have the time to handle the problem personally.
3. The community is summoned to ask for their assistance. The twelve instruct them, *"seek out **from among you** seven men of good reputation, full of the Holy Spirit and wisdom, whom we may appoint over this business;"*
4. Having given this assignment, the apostles continue in prayer and ministry.
5. Fellow congregants choose the seven.
6. The apostles lay hands on those overseeing this ministry and **release** them.
7. The Word of God spreads, the number of disciples multiplies, and *"a great many of the priests were obedient to the faith."*

These men were selected because the apostles needed to stay focused on their calling. The Kingdom of God was growing exponentially in the wake of Pentecost. Facing such strong demands on their time, it was necessary to pass the baton to the coming generation of leaders. Remarkably, the apostles assign this task to their lay leaders.

This serves as an excellent model for designating point persons to assist in the ministry of the church. The listing of this chosen group of seven commences with two highly influential leaders—Stephen and Philip. These two laymen are about to become the centerpieces for the outpouring of God's Spirit in Acts 6, 7, and 8. Our Lord will use them as unmistakable manifestations of God's favor given to those who are obedient to His calling and willing to serve.

The job requirements call for mature leadership, but the selection process is altogether new. Overseeing the allotment for the widows will require the assistance of men of great faith, full of wisdom and the Holy Spirit. The apostolic fathers simply instruct their brethren how to choose the best candidates. Their peers know whom to choose and they are delighted with the freedom given to them by the apostles. If you will, the seven are given their own "fishing vessel."

The Outpouring Begins

Just how did God initiate this mutually beneficial process between Jews and Gentiles? The stage was set during the Old Testament, as Jews were set apart. Then, with Jesus' appearance, God reveals the details of His plans to bring both peoples back together. One of the clearest signs of these events, foreshadowed in the Old Covenant, takes place here in Acts 6. Let's start with the timeline preceding Acts 6 for a brief overview.

From the day God called Abram (later Abraham) to leave his homeland and follow God, the Lord's plan has been to see His children, beginning with those of Jewish heritage, come to faith. Pentecost, falling on Shavuot, is the convergent unifying confirmation of both old and new covenants, as well as the Trinity. God promised in the old; Yeshua appears in the new, He dies, He's resurrected; and the Holy Spirit was poured out. Father, Son, and Holy Spirit. Following Pentecost God forges one new humanity.

A close inspection of the Lord's blueprint for unity unveils a pattern for establishing ministries equipped to release *dunamis* (Kingdom-building power) for ministry outreach. At Pentecost, the Lord demonstrates a release of His Holy Spirit that is capable of changing the spiritual landscape for *any* community.

A greatly condensed view of the first ten chapters of the Book of Acts takes us from the time of our Lord's resurrection through the fulfilled promise of power by the Holy Spirit, and ultimately to other nations beyond the boundaries of Israel. Kindly keep in mind what will happen when we apply this hope of salvation to our contemporary Kingdom circumstances.

Acts chapter 2 shows us the miraculous outpouring of the Holy Spirit. The crippled man at the Gate Beautiful stands up for the first time in his life after Peter and John pray for him. These two are arrested, challenged by the Sanhedrin, and warned about their faith, for which they are jubilant.

In Acts 3 and 4 the apostles move out boldly to proclaim the gospel. Nothing will dissuade them. Undaunted by threats, the apostles continue to witness their strong faith; only to be imprisoned, then miraculously released by an angel of the Lord. The apostles have seen the resurrected Lord. The church is mushrooming. They are unconquerable by any foe!

In the wake of this unprecedented flow of the Holy Spirit, the Lord is closely monitoring the behavior of the newcomers to the church. Acts chapter 5 uncovers a heretofore unheard of level of accountability. Ananias and Sapphira selfishly abuse the bounds of appropriate offerings by falsely and vainly proclaiming their generosity. Each in turn literally drops dead at the altar and is hauled out of the house of worship.

An awesome fear of a Holy God is manifested among the saints. This is no longer a show of piety; this is a life-and-death happening. The Holy Spirit will not be trifled with and there will be no counterfeit spirituality!

By this time, Gamaliel, Saul's pharisaical mentor, sees fit to advise his compatriots that these outspoken testimonies of the apostles will not stand the test of time unless they are following God. Surprisingly, Gamaliel counsels that there is no reason to resist their teachings.

This directive accomplishes two significant results. First, it appeases the Sanhedrin's insistence that these Messianic zealots were exaggerating their claims about Yeshua and should be confronted and contained. Second, it defused some of the growing animosity and jealousy within the Jewish community that could easily lead to a death sentence, something that Saul would soon be acting out. We can't help but notice that the apostles on trial rejoiced that they were counted worthy to suffer punishment!

What follows on the heels of Acts 2 through 5, manifested by this outpouring of the Holy Spirit, accompanied by signs and wonders and an unquenchable desire by the apostles to share their faith, is a seemingly inconsequential assignment for a select group. One of the ministries in need of assistance was the daily distribution of food to the Hellenistic widows of the faith.

At this moment is the tipping point in time when the Lord begins to recruit an army of lay leaders. The apostles seek aid from seven elders. God has determined to release these chosen saints into a fresh manifestation of His favor. The Bible's magnificent seven are commissioned.

Contrasting Calls

In stark contrast to the fresh move of the Holy Spirit upon Stephen and Philip, we watch the startling transformation of Saul, who both aids and directs Stephen's martyrdom. Saul is dead set on persecuting the advocates of Yeshua and is headed out of town to inflict more damage on his perceived enemies. His headstrong ways cause him to become oblivious to the coming Kingdom of God. The Lord knocks Saul off his donkey and blinds him. God had seen and heard enough of Saul's doctrinal zealousness. He intends to use Saul's passion for a higher calling.

Imagine Saul's heartbreak upon realizing that his efforts are in direct opposition to God's will. Consider how distraught he must have been as he recalled the stoning of one of the Lord's chosen vessels. The blindness of Saul's eyes was eclipsed by the pain in his heart for his headstrong disobedience to God.

Surely this realization must have galvanized Saul's ministry from that day forward. There would never be a threat that could topple Saul's (soon to be Paul's) evangelistic ministry. How could he ever complain after overseeing the death of God's anointed? Paul would never look back in doubt after this course-altering catharsis.

But, like Saul becoming Paul, those seven selected to assist in the widows' sustenance will lay the groundwork for an unprecedented move of God's sovereign purposes. A close examination of Stephen and Philip aids us in appreciating the release of mature lay leaders.

Stephen, full of the Holy Spirit, is featured in the balance of Acts 6 and 7 as he ministers to the traditional Jewish leadership. Before his demise, Stephen witnesses the heavens open and Jesus sitting at the right hand of God. He is subsequently stoned to death under Saul's condemning eye.

Philip answers the Holy Spirit's call to preach the gospel to an Ethiopian eunuch studying the Book of Isaiah—the first distinct biblical reference of a Gentile to hear the gospel message and come to faith. Philip is immediately translated 25 miles up the Mediterranean coast where he enters Samaria preaching the gospel.

May we all be blessed to have Stephens and Philips in the ministries God gives us to steward the needy. Ironically, nothing further is spoken about the needs of the widows in Acts 6.

Stephen and Philip are part of an eldership of seven. They have had hands laid on them by the apostles and are then released into ministry. They have accepted the ministry call to *"walk worthy of the calling with which you were called"* (Ephesians 4:1).

Selecting the Seven

These men were selected because the apostles needed to stay focused on their calling. The Kingdom of God was growing exponentially in the wake of Pentecost. Facing such strong demands on their time, it was necessary to pass the baton to the coming generation of leaders. This is reminiscent of our prior description of Jethro's counsel to Moses to delegate leadership.

I would be remiss if I failed to point out a strong parallel between the time crunch faced by these patriarchs and the overburdened job description of today's pastors. Our shepherds are lacking such apostolic mentorship. There are few places to turn for wise counsel. If you are upset with your leader, kindly take into account the degree of exposure to criticism your reverend faces. There are too many hats to wear and too many tasks that should be delegated. Pastors are working within a revised system that does not provide essential support. Pray for your pastor.

Choosing the seven called for mature leadership, but the selection process is altogether new. Overseeing the allotment for Hellenistic widows (those of Greek heritage) will require the assistance of men of great faith, full of wisdom and the Holy Spirit. The apostles simply instruct their brethren how to choose the best candidates. Their peers know whom to choose, and they are delighted with the freedom given to them by their leaders.

Verse 5 confirms their approval: *"The proposal pleased the whole group."* Please don't pass by this remarkable statement without a significant pause. The leaders of the burgeoning church have just handed authority over a ministry to laymen. And what's more, this unprecedented move *pleased the whole group.*

This unity is entirely uncharacteristic of contemporary churches.

It is not often that spiritual authority is transferred without protest. When leaders are approached with problems, even the wisest solutions usually beg for criticism from some faction or those who have been marginalized. Not so in this situation. This unity is entirely uncharacteristic of contemporary churches.

Leadership has been offered to laymen and everyone is happy. This feat pinpoints the *tipping point* of the New Testament. Those with authority allow their flock of followers to step out to make their own selections and then to encourage them. Are we listening? What just happened?

In a word, *release!* Imagine the explosive growth of the Kingdom of God as His saints are released to fulfill their calling. This answers the heart cry that God has deposited within each of us. Since we are made in His image, there is a passion within us that must be fulfilled.

That passion took our Savior to the cross. That passion brings great men to their knees. That passion gives a battle-wearied soldier the courage to charge through enemy gunfire. That passion is the force that drives us to carry forward the gospel, regardless of the cost. "Dear God, release the saints!"

When I contemplate this passage of Scripture, my thoughts go to the great quote by Henry David Thoreau, "The mass of men lead lives of quiet desperation." There is an additive to this insight not attributed to Thoreau: "and go to the grave having never sung their song." Whoever tagged this to the end of this famous quote certainly understood the brokenness of humanity. As leaders in the Kingdom, it's our responsibility to see to it that this quote jolts us awake and stirs our spirits.

Most leaders realize that it's their responsibility to equip the saints. Yet, even those leaders who see the value of equipping as the purpose of discipling seldom reach the *tipping point*—the place of release. We dare not partially prepare our people. Disciples under the guidance and authority of a mighty man or woman of God need to hear them reiterate the word Yeshua gave us, "Go!"

Priests Become Obedient

> *Then the word of God spread, and the number of the disciples multiplied greatly in Jerusalem, and a great many of the priests were obedient to the faith* (Acts 6:7).

The result of the groundswell of the Holy Spirit in Acts 6 causes such an outpouring of miracles and evangelism that the priests change their ways. We are accustomed to think of ministry from a corporate perspective—from the top down. But this is clearly a case for the gospel being spread from the bottom up. The lay people, having been released by the apostolic leadership, are showing the priests a thing or two—God is answering their prayers.

Notice it says, *"and a great many of the priests were obedient to the faith."* That comment stops me dead in my tracks. This is far more than a tag at the end of a passage in the Bible. Think of all the leaders who have grown cold because they have not seen a move of the Spirit. How many await the coming awakening, not knowing that the answer to its release will come by releasing their saints? They know the Kingdom of God is near; not knowing it's inside their sanctuaries!

> *And He Himself gave some to be apostles, some prophets, some evangelists, and some pastors and teachers, for the equipping of the saints for the work of ministry, for the edifying of the body of Christ,* **till we all come to the unity of the faith** *and of the knowledge of the Son of God, to a perfect man, to the measure of the stature of the fullness of Christ; that we should no longer be children, tossed to and fro and carried about with every wind of doctrine, by the trickery of men, in the cunning craftiness of deceitful plotting, but, speaking the truth in love, may grow up in all things into Him who is the head—Christ—from whom the whole body,* **joined and knit together by what every joint supplies,** *according to the effective working by which every part does its share, causes growth of the body for the edifying of itself in love* (Ephesians 4:11-16).

Our contemporary church is crumbling under the weight of top-down, pastor-directed ministry lacking the guidance of elders, apostles, deacons, and prophets. Unless we humbly serve as Christ served the church and gave His life for her, we are not fulfilling our calling. By promoting divisional doctrines as the avenue to our identity, we trip over the line that keeps us secured to the mooring cleats edging the dock. Yes, our ship looks great, but we can't feed the masses in port.

Unless we cast off and head for deep waters,
our bait cutting and filling of oil jars won't
help us a bit.

Unless we cast off and head for deep waters, our bait cutting and filling of oil jars won't help us a bit. This is humankind trying to reprioritize God's fishing boat into our own life rafts. We can sit passively on the pier and bicker about how to tie a bowline, or proactively untie the mooring line and snap on our oilcloth. Combining our talents for navigation, setting sails, and dropping nets yields glorious gains. Let's send aloft our youngsters with the best vision to locate seagulls circling the big schools near the surface. With good teamwork, we can feed thousands, just like Jesus.

It's time to build ministries that impact our communities. In cases like this, the lay members of our congregations will take up their mantles. On that day, our contemporary Stephens and Philips will execute proper conduct as fishers of men, according to Jesus' model for ministry. On that day, His church and His priests will reawaken to the move of the Holy Spirit and become *obedient to the faith*. Just as in Acts 6, the tipping point will shift, the outpouring will be magnificent, and the church will again become attractive.

An "attractive" church supplies fruit that lasts. It's how we show the world we are His disciples. All this effort we put into making a seeker-sensitive church with coffee bars inside the church foyer. Why not take a neighbor out for coffee? Acts of lovingkindness preach the good news better than the newspaper. Yes, we have a love for each other that shines from within. How does that compare to the brilliance that radiates from a united church that loves her community? Just what are we trying to prove? Are we doing this for the benefit of others, or for ourselves?

False identities are hypocritical, competitive, and divisive. They don't make us one. The body of Yeshua is only as healthy as it is unified. With tens of thousands of church bodies, we are scattered, isolated, and ineffective. While we are thinking about whom to take for tea, how about asking someone from a different church? We have much in common and we just might learn something from each other.

Today's church has suffered mightily by trying to build leaders who follow us, not Him. Those who follow the King build the Kingdom. God is looking for leaders who are intent on following Him and equipping others to do the same. The test of this model comes by putting service where it belongs—as the uppermost call of doctrine. Lovingkindness fulfills Messiah's commandment.

> *How precious is Your lovingkindness, O God! Therefore the children of men put their trust under the shadow of Your wings. They are abundantly satisfied with the fullness of Your house, and You give them drink from the river of Your pleasures. For with You is the fountain of life; in Your light we see light.*

This passage is from Psalm 36. What should we do with God's lovingkindness? Receive it; then share it with everyone. In *"the fullness of Your house"* He provides us with *"drink from the river of Your pleasures."* Would you like that with cream and sugar?

The One that Got Away

One good nudge, that's all it takes for a life to change forever. I don't know where your "button" is located. This button is the one that activates a human being to start making a difference. It's the button that says, "I'm tired of being an observer or critic of what's wrong with this world, and I'm doing something about it."

A person who walks in freedom is one who takes action when he or she sees something is out of place and responds by helping. It can be picking up a piece of trash on the street where you live and disposing of it properly. It may be sitting with someone who is grieving the loss of a loved one. Or it may be adopting a foster child who is headed toward a dead end.

Freedom protects what we've received from God; not taking

what's "owed" to us by humanity. If we demand our "fair share," we move into justification. There is no end to that trail. Justice must be weighed on a supernatural scale. In the natural, the best we can do is to compensate. We won't ever determine how much is enough. Thankfully, we know the difference between not doing our best and fulfillment in God's economy.

I remember the one good nudge that got my course corrected toward God. I attended a conference where people were learning life skills. I had taken a pledge that I would not divulge the content of the meetings. I soon discovered this promise was part of a very effective marketing scheme, enticing people to register for a training regimen run by this self-help organization. The program was very pricey. Even the elevated cost added to the mystique that something was being taught of extreme value.

Toward the end of training, after several days in this intensive environment with exercises to improve our self-image, all of the attendees were ushered into a large room. One of our instructors asked for a volunteer. He did not explain what the request would be.

"Who are you?"

A brave woman raised her hand. The teacher asked her to stand and identify herself, "Who are you?" As the woman began to answer the question, the teacher cut her off and asked her again, "Who are you?" The woman hesitated, and then started to answer the question the second time. Before she had said finished giving her name, the teacher cut her short again, "Who are you?"

This cycle was repeated about five or six times. The woman struggled to find the right words to properly respond while the rest of us in the room squirmed with discomfort, very glad that we had not been so foolish as to be the guinea pig. I recall thinking that this was not a proper reward for being courageous enough to raise her hand. This lady was being sucker punched in public, but she had offered, so it was her own fault.

I'm convinced the teacher would have pestered anyone who had volunteered in exactly the same fashion. The lesson to be garnered from this exercise appeared to be, when someone gets in your face and challenges you, or your identity, you need to be able to rise to the occasion and stand up to even aggressive criticism. Assert yourself. Don't let the world define your personality. Rise up.

Well, we all sat there stunned, as the instructor became more adamant, "Who are you?" The woman started to crack. The teacher was heartless. Perhaps he thought it was acceptable to tear down another person's identity for the sake of teaching the class some great lesson on assertiveness.

Every time the woman tried to dig deeper into her inner person, to meet the challenge, the teacher raised his voice louder to denounce her attempts to overcome his demand for her identity. This was agonizing to behold.

I clearly remembered that I cringed, along with the rest of the audience, as we watched this woman being verbally abused. It became very clear that no answer this woman was going to give would satisfy the instructor. We were learning the hard way the necessity to stand on your own two feet, even under such a withering attack, and press on with your life's purpose. This was their way of demonstrating the importance of being unshakeable.

There probably were some hearty folks in this crowd of a couple hundred who would have stood up to the teacher and proclaimed their identity boldly to the world. There are some of us who are built that way. But this example required a member of the audience to stand her ground as the person with the microphone publicly humiliated her. The instructor in front of us was the authority in that room. What could we do? I thought this example was pitiful, callous, uncalled for.

The woman broke down in tears and collapsed back into her seat. Several of those nearby tentatively reached to comfort her, but did so furtively, watching the teacher to see if, by tending to the volunteer, they too would be singled out.

Something within me went off. I had decided to disconnect my emotions from this event, so I sat back and watched this woman being treated inhumanely. Oh, it was easy to justify my passivity. After all, this was a learning environment. It was only a lesson, not a "true life experience." Since this was a classroom situation during a closed session, we could take certain liberties—all in the name of giving a lesson on taking charge.

Basic training in the military has many similar moments when the drill instructor gets right up in your face, nose to nose, and shouts out questions and orders to make his point so clearly that you shutter to think what will happen if you don't answer properly. And until you shout out, "Sir, Yes Sir!" in harmony with every member of the platoon in taut attention with muscles flexed and chest thrust out, there would be no peace. The DI would never be satisfied until his squad had been broken to the degree that they understood every possible response other than to give your life for the sake of every member of the platoon, was the wrong answer. The only right reply was to be willing to die protecting the life, honor, and dignity of another soldier.

But this wasn't the military. By signing our pledge, we had agreed to being treated in an unusual manner. Of course, when we registered we didn't think we'd be facing anything like this. We were in a nice hotel. It appeared to be a safe place. We came to learn life skills. Character crushing didn't appear on the menu.

After this exercise in humility, which is the nicest way I can describe this public disgrace, I looked at this woman sitting in her seat. The room had cleared out. Everyone was anxious to leave. By now several of her compatriots had come around her to comfort her. But she was defeated, hurt, sobbing.

I tried talking to some of the guys I had befriended during the course of this training. The general consensus was that this woman needed to take control of the situation and tell the teacher to stick it where the sun doesn't shine. And since she had volunteered, she had forfeited her right to self-protection.

I was shocked. I remember one of my acquaintances was a rabbi.

I looked to him, anticipating his commiserating with the victim of this dressing down. No such luck. His attitude was, "This girl just needs to get it together and take a stand." I began to realize that the general response for this audience was passive. No one wanted this to happen to him or her. As long as it was someone else, then although it was painful, that was their learning curve and they would learn to survive.

I went home that night and couldn't sleep. I realized that I had betrayed that woman. I had decided to stay anonymous. I was going to blend into the crowd and observe. I had reduced myself to be as inconspicuous as possible because I didn't want to be the next one to be put on the hot seat. All the while thinking, "If they call on me, I'll be tough as nails. I'll stand up for myself. They'll never get me to back down."

But that wasn't working. I remember thinking back on my childhood. I was brought up in a home with solid values. I knew that people needed to be helped. Some people needed to be protected, especially those at risk. It didn't matter that we were in a classroom that afternoon. That woman was being humiliated and every person in the room, especially myself, sat in horror, afraid to step in.

I did not man up. I did not stand up and advise the instructor to back off. I did not protect a woman who was no longer able to defend herself. I was not the man I was raised to be. A defender stands for what is right. I stayed seated. I could have protected her, but I let the opportunity slip away. Woe is me.

That was my good nudge. That was the moment when I knew if I continued to live this way I was never going to be the man God had called me to be. As I said, something shoved me off balance. I'd had enough hypocrisy that said it was OK to abuse someone if there was a higher purpose to be achieved. That type of thinking did not fit my persona. And if I decided to think that way, I would forfeit the high calling on my life. Something was stirring inside that could not be denied any longer.

That something is the genuine heart of the person who is willing to give up his own life and his own well-being in order to protect a victim. It was that incident that lead me to Jesus. That was the good nudge. That woman, a person whom I never met, a person whom I never saw again, needed help and I didn't move a muscle.

I couldn't live with myself. I had failed to assist someone in her time of need. It didn't matter how many other people were in the room; I was silent when it was time to speak up. That life course really did do me a lot of good, but not in the way they had designed it. What it taught me was humanity's techniques for self-reliance and overcoming challenges are fatally flawed.

> *When we justify passivity in the face of injustice, then everyone suffers.*

These activities were creating scenarios that caused individuals to justify putting their own life in front of others. Survival justified all behaviors. The willingness to sacrifice our own well-being that others might gain was viewed as flawed and foolish. This was not what I believe God put us here for. When we justify passivity in the face of injustice, then everyone suffers.

The victim suffers. The perpetrator suffers. The observer suffers. The world suffers. God suffers. A person fulfilled is a person who unflinchingly takes a stand for righteousness. That's what gets us out of bed early. That's what makes us do what needs to be done, even when no one else knows what we're doing. It's the right thing to do. That's all we truly need to know.

What will it take to give you one good nudge? Don't let your next opportunity be "The One that Got Away."

Chapter 17

Getting Out of the Boat

Releasing Authority

Returning to Acts 6, there is much to learn from this simple, yet profound, example of those willing to answer the call to serve. This appointed eldership is established over a geographic region. As chosen deacons, they represent leadership that is based upon calling, not the shifting whims or waves of constrained doctrine. The widows' cry for help was not reinterpreted through the lens of a predetermined prejudice, merely designed to protect the lofty position of the priesthood. As with the good Samaritan, the first apostles were sensitive to a need and they acted accordingly.

The apostles released the seven. They placed that missional outreach into very capable hands. These men were known, respected, and trusted. When they took over the reins of this ministry, they were given authority over more than just food distribution. They were given authority over the region as well. The resulting explosion of outreach tells us of their impact. In every church sits a tipping point, most often dormant, awaiting a righteous nudge by a righteous judge.

Unlike a typical denominational eldership in our Western world, which is not centrally located within a region, these selected seven are both locally situated and locally overseen by a counsel that represents the *entire* body of the church. This is a simple, effective, God-ordained model for regional authority.

We are cognizant our enemy assaults certain regions. Strife over the City of David is forever fierce. Ezra and Nehemiah struggled to restore its walls. Historically, control over Jerusalem has changed hands dozens and dozens of times. This battle never fails to punctuate the evening headlines. We know our enemy wants authority over geographical areas. Yet the church fails to consolidate forces within cities, states, or nations. Our lack of unity exposes us to diabolical schemes.

> *For we do not wrestle against flesh and blood, but against principalities, against powers, against the rulers of the darkness of this age, against spiritual hosts of wickedness in the heavenly places* (Ephesians 6:12).

The first apostles governed the spiritual well-being of those located within their same region, specifically Jerusalem. They became aware of a local problem via firsthand knowledge. Leaders were swiftly chosen and called to deal with it. We can't overlook the fact that their peers were already familiar with the hearts' desires for the seven. This was reflected in the Lord's release of favor.

These men were not selected based upon denominational values, but upon their willingness to serve. They were called to address the most significant problem facing the ministry at that time. What's more, they were all filled with the Holy Spirit. Here's a working model of the church placing loving service as the highest order of the day. The results speak for themselves 2,000 years later.

Territorial Disputes

Examining dominions of authority on earth commonly reflect geographic topography. We find corresponding ways of defining territory in culture. Scientific mapping identifies layers and regions. Sociopolitical divisions determine borders. Economics both define and divide us. Yes, even race and religion cause further breakdown.

Add the societal cross section of history, laws, rules, wars, families, nations, and the list goes on. On top of this are invisible areas of spiritual hierarchy. Each arena offers benefits and barriers.

Whether we face a predator or a territorial dispute, what holds true for people also holds true for fish. Larger animals are stronger, carry more weight, and tend to bully their way around to gain ground. So we need to be aware of both the region we enter and its governing strongholds before we exercise our spiritual authority. Likewise, fishing for men requires a lot of wisdom.

Striking out into the deep requires an understanding of the magnitude of territorial dominion. Fish respond to the same stimuli in deep waters as they do in the shallows. They are drawn to food, yet they are still wary of predators.

When we step out in faith to witness our relationship with Yeshua, we have to realize we are stepping into territory where our enemy has grown accustomed to rule. Lines of spiritual authority are extended when we bring forth the gospel. There will be a battle for souls. Nevertheless, Yeshua promised us the gates of hell shall not prevail against us, because we bring a just and righteous cause.

> *It takes hard work to conquer our foes.*
> *Fortunately, the battle belongs to the Lord,*
> *but the victory is ours!*

There is much more to this war than witnessing. We are taking on spiritual hosts that have occupied certain territories. Although we are the highest authority, our adversary has established strongholds for generations. It takes hard work to conquer our foes. Fortunately, the battle belongs to the Lord, but the victory is ours!

Jacob's Joint

Jacob wrestled through the dark hours with the Angel of God. Jacob refused to let go unless the Angel blessed him. He's unwilling to relinquish his grip on the Heavenly Host, so the Angel touches Jacob's hip, causing the ligament to tear. Jacob finally lets go.

Jacob's hip comes out of joint, forcing him to walk with a limp. At this moment the Angel gives Jacob his new name—"Israel." Israel describes one who struggles with God. That dislocation changed Israel's gait and characterized his new identity. Likewise, when the State of Israel receives her Messiah Yeshua and is restored to wholeness, *"it will be as life from the dead"* (Romans 11:15; 6:4).

That miraculous salvation of the Jews will bring God's healing touch to Israel's torn ligament. At that moment the bones of spiritual Israel will be pulled back into perfect alignment. On that day the body of believers, Jews and Gentiles, will move and breathe and have its being in Yeshua. When this happens, the nation Israel, whose name was once Jacob, will be fully restored by the love of God.

> *but, speaking the truth in love, may grow up in all things into Him who is the head—Christ—from whom the whole body, joined and knit together by what every joint supplies, according to the effective working by which every part does its share, causes growth of the body for the edifying of itself in love* (Ephesians 4:15-16).

We must reacquaint ourselves with Romans chapter 11, as its meaning is unfolding right in front of our eyes. The church has debated Paul's message to Rome for centuries. But that was prior to Israel regaining her Promised Land and returning her capital to Jerusalem. This has silenced much of the theological debate that occurred during the era when the Jews were scattered around the globe.

Ongoing arguments persist, despite the fact that possession of the land has been accomplished, but the focus has shifted to disagreements about Israel's methods of survival. Israel is a stumbling block to those who refuse to accept her ongoing role in the Kingdom of God. God made an everlasting covenant with Israel. While this may upset many, God's covenant will never be broken.

After two millennia we have finally entered the season of the fullness of the Gentiles. Ever so slowly the church is coming to realize it's calling to embrace Israel. In our day, as the veil is being lifted off of Israel, as Jew and Gentile become one in Messiah Yeshua, as the one new man emerges, Israel is beginning to see her promised Messiah. That nation and all nations under God rejoice in the harmony of growing together, edifying each other in love.

One new man characterizes the shared identity of Jewish and Gentile believers who accept Yeshua as Head. Alas, the Lord is getting His first glimpse of His bride. She will be dressed in fine linens, pure and white. She will exude lovingkindness. And she will not limp!

Transition: Getting Out of the Boat

Transition is the great faith builder. Ask a woman who is giving birth. Her body insists that she have a child. Contractions are not voluntary. They come whenever they come. This child is going to be born and this mother's life must yield to this all-encompassing event.

There is some relief. Resting between pushes. Mopping mom's brow. Sucking on ice chips. Receiving encouragement. Daddy or doc can speak comforting words. But most of the time it is hard work, or getting ready to work. About the only thing the woman can control is her breathing and how hard she decides to push. This is an irreversible pathway. There is no round trip. The woman is in transition.

Going through transition is actually a process of losing control. There are few things in life that make us as uncomfortable as losing control. Our toughest moments occur when we try to resist something that is just too big for us to maneuver.

We can shout and scream. We can beg or plead. We can clench our fists. But we're not in control. We're in transition. It's time to yield. It's God's agenda, not ours. We suffer from believing we have far more control over life than we actually do.

There are divine timelines that govern the universe. Part of our walk of faith is to learn how to recognize and accept the sovereign moves of God. Father God is operating on a grand scale. *"But when the fullness of time had come, God sent forth His Son, born of woman"* (Galatians 4:4).

Although we don't like the process, it's during transition that we learn the most about God and about ourselves. The story of the Holy Scriptures is the story of humanity in transition. Every parable spoken demonstrates God's sovereignty and the results of our following His leading, or trying to do things under our own power.

God does not change. And God's Son *Yeshua is the same yesterday, today, and forever* (Hebrews 13:8). So the simple process of determining who's in charge leaves only one participant remaining. Guess which party needs to change in balancing the equation that leads to a successful life? Right. We are the variable.

This is not to say that God is unyielding. But the Lord will only adjust our horizons as the result of righteous requests and willful submission to His ways. We aren't going to fool God and it is foolish to try. But when transition comes, and it comes to all, we will resist change with every fiber of our being. It won't be long until that newborn babe reaches his second birthday and decides he doesn't want to go to bed. That's a preview of humanity pushing against God's authority to get our own way.

What about those who appear to always get their own way— the ones who bully and demand? And let's not forget the victims of cruelty and inhumanity. Don't worry; God hasn't overlooked anything. He knows exactly what we're going through. There is an accounting for every thought, deed, and action. In the fullness of time, our Lord will act to set everything in order. As we wait for things to happen, we are in transition. And transition is a great builder of faith. Fullness is the fruit of faith.

Faith is the bridge that allows us to reach our destiny. *All things are possible for one who believes!* (Mark 9:23). So God places us deep into situations that force us to exercise the muscle of our faith. Our King likes us strong.

One of the best examples of someone in transition begins in John chapter 13 as we observe Peter trying to respond to Yeshua's decision to wash His disciple's feet. He protests, *"Master, are you going to wash my feet?"*

Peter is now in transition. Note Yeshua's response. *"You don't know what I'm doing now, but you will understand after these things."* For all of Peter's desire to serve his Rabbi, it was unfathomable that Yeshua would become a servant to Peter. He tells Peter, the one whom He calls the rock upon whom He will build His church, that the fisherman is not capable of comprehending what He is up to.

Peter will have nothing to do with it. He adamantly refuses to allow Yeshua to wash his feet, *"You shall never wash my feet."* Note Peter's insistence on taking control of a situation that Yeshua tells him he doesn't understand. That doesn't stop Peter. It's not until Yeshua lays out the ground rules that Peter yields.

Yeshua tells Peter, *"If I don't wash you, you have no part with me."* The Lord is making it known that Peter's demands will not get him what he wants. Peter capitulates. In fact, his submission is more than Yeshua asks. Simon Peter said to Him, *"Master, then not only my feet, but also my hands and my head!"*

Yeshua explains He has already made Peter and the disciples clean, so all that needs to be done is to wash their feet. By completing this act of lovingkindness, Yeshua shows His followers how it is that a Teacher who represents God is supposed to teach others. This act of complete humility sets a standard for service that totally redefines the role of teaching disciples.

Watching Peter's transition tells us much about ourselves. For people to be drawn to a man of God means they need to see their leader humble himself before those who follow him. That's a tall order.

Yeshua had to exemplify lovingkindness through action, not just words. He chose the moment in the Seder when the leader cleanses himself at the onset of the meal to wash the feet of his followers. Such a model of leadership had never been contemplated. Of course Peter would have objected. He wanted His Master to be admired, not scorned. Peter had yet to see what Yeshua was about to suffer.

What appears to be the obvious course to glorify his Master did not get the expected result. God is the One who will glorify Yeshua. Peter was right in wanting to honor his Master. But it was not for Peter to determine how God is to serve His followers. This is highly significant because the foot washing shows us that God is willing to do far more than we can imagine in demonstrating His love for us.

Before the chapter is completed, Yeshua will caution Peter, who pleads with his Leader, *"Master, why can't I follow You now? I'll lay down my life for you."*

And Yeshua must again take Peter deeper into his transition. The Lord informs him that Peter will deny Him three times. Peter's resistance shows us that our devotion to God will cost us much more than we can measure. After Yeshua's resurrection, as He encounters the fishermen back at work at the Sea of Tiberius, He will meet the discouraged Peter and fully restore him.

Knowing all the efforts Yeshua would go through to exemplify God's profound love for Peter, we start to appreciate why Yeshua encouraged him to get out of the boat. Peter had great faith.

> *We need to learn how to use this supernatural gift of faith to glorify God. When we do, all things are possible!*

Peter's problem is the same as ours—we need to learn how to use this supernatural gift of faith to glorify God. When we do, all things are possible: *without faith it is impossible to please God* (Hebrews 11:6).

God was pleased when Peter asked if he could come to Him on the water. Our Majesty's pleasure is the *Ruach HaKodesh*, the Wind of the Holy Spirit that kept Peter from sinking.

Having faith is only the beginning. Having faith in Yeshua as the One whom God sent is the ultimate release. It's one thing to be released back *into* the water. It's something of an entirely different dimension to walk *upon* those waters.

But the good news doesn't stop there. The best news is that God wants each of us to experience the same supernatural blessing He gave to His apostle Peter. God wants us to exercise our faith too.

Our boat, our ministry, our calling will one day ask us to walk on the water. Be glad, because it is for our King's glory that we will shine like stars in the heavens on the day He beckons. God will take us through the transition to bring us to Him.

Chapter 18

Here Comes the Bride

Bodybuilding for Unity

When we divide God's church, we build Babel again. We need to be bodybuilding for unity. That's joining the ligaments together so that each part of the body works in divine order, supplying what is needed for the entire body to be edified under the headship of Yeshua. That's a simple image to hold on to.

What good does it do to only exercise one muscle? And how arrogant is it to claim that our denomination represents all the muscles in the body? Absurd. God intentionally distributes His gifts far and wide. We are shortchanging our King if we limit our service to just our local church, a particular denomination, or a large independent church. Furthermore, building a network of churches that claim a unique status in the Kingdom of God is outside of our Lord's wishes. The inevitable consequence of such thinking is divisive. Strength comes from acceptance of everyone who names Yeshua as Lord and Savior.

Those who share occupancy in God's household of faith are expected to fellowship with other parts of our Lord's body. The only alternative maintains that others are less than equal parts of the body. That's where wars come from. We cannot expect theological debates to come up with all the answers. When we get shoulder-to-shoulder in problem solving for ministry, those debates quickly fade into the background. When love, acceptance, and forgiveness are the guidelines of our faith, theological walls start to crumble.

Let there be no divisions among you (1 Corinthians 1:10).

A unified church places service above all doctrinal differences. Ministry brings everyone to the foot of the cross on even footing. That honors the oft-repeated doctrine that God loves us all the same. That's Kingdom life. That's becoming His bride. That's what God designed us for. That's whom God is longing to see. That's whom God is asking us to be.

Doctrine has its place, but we err by trying to sculpt it into our identity. My identity is in Yeshua, the One who died for me. Doctrine is essential for deeper understanding, but if we believe our doctrine is superior to another's, we divide what God has instructed us to keep as one. In so doing, we ignore Jesus' final, poignant prayer. These were His last words before going to the cross. He prayed for us. He prayed for you and for me. He prayed that you and I would be one, *"that the world may know that You [God] have sent Me, and have loved them as You [God] have loved Me"* (John 17:23).

Yeshua promised us we would have the same relationship with God as He has—if we act according to His heart's deepest desire—that we would be one! And the world drives by our churches, not knowing or caring that we know the living God. Why should they stop? They don't know us. They haven't seen us in loving action.

What did Saint Peter teach us? *Love covers over a multitude of sins* (1 Peter 4:8 NIV). He ought to know. Look what Yeshua taught him so he would be a fisher of men.

God made you and me to be bodybuilders of His church. Let's build a healthy body!

Those who follow the King build His Kingdom. God is looking for leaders who are intent on following Him and building others to do the same. That's whom God made you and me to be—bodybuilders of His church. Let's build a healthy body.

Righteous Acts

At the instant of our salvation, the Holy Spirit sparks a unique segment within our once-dormant DNA to fulfill its destiny. We are programmed to recognize righteousness when we see it. Our heart's desire is to travel this highway of holiness. This is our spiritual destiny. A burly biker or loathsome linebacker is putty before such purity.

In fact, it appears God is not coming for His bride until she is performing the service for which she has been called. This is true religion. This is living out a mature relationship within the community where we have been planted. This is how the bride makes herself ready for her groom—*righteous acts!*

Is this not the path God has chosen for us? Release into missional outreach precipitates the reign of God's undying favor. In this atmosphere we can let down our nets for a real catch. We can stand before judges and juries. When called to educate the existing establishment, we can personify the righteousness of Stephen and Philip in response to the move of the Holy Ghost. We can even walk on water.

> *Our gift is unique; it's not duplicable, it's our identity, our spiritual fingerprint, our holy DNA. It's why we are born, and then born again.*

God has put the ministry that glorifies Him within the heart of every saint. He wants us to perform, according to His calling. As apostles, prophets, evangelists, teachers, and pastors, we have been gifted, that we might share our gifts with the saints, and then release them. That gift is unique to each and every person here on earth. It's not duplicable, it's our identity, our spiritual fingerprint, our holy DNA. It's why we are born, and then born again.

The model of church we portray in conferences, in media, and church growth seminars is often fashioned to point the saints toward ministry inside the four walls of church. Without realizing our shortsightedness, we expect our parishioners to follow shepherds like sheep. The gifts God gives us are to equip the sheep to follow Him, not us!

Think of the talents God gives to us. One day we will stand before Him and He will ask us to make an accounting of what we have done with the gifts He has so generously put into our hands. That parable is a foreshadowing of our encounter with the living Lord in the heavenly realm (Matthew 25:14-30).

Or consider the five virgins with jars of oil, who stood ready to fill their lamps in joyful expectation of our King's return for His bride. Initially ten virgins awaited the coming king, but only five had oil (Matthew 25:1-13). That oil is the anointing that comes from fulfilling God's calling on our lives by faithfully applying the gifts for which we were created. To miss this opportunity is equivalent to a bride not picking out a wedding gown for her own marriage!

Fine Linens

> *"Let us be glad and rejoice and give Him glory, for the marriage of the Lamb has come, and His wife has made herself ready." And to her it was granted to be arrayed in fine linen, clean and bright,* **for the fine linen is the righteous acts of the saints** (Revelation 19:7-8).

The Lord is looking for a bride who is involved in righteous acts—missional outreach emphasizing service to those in our communities who are in need. This will require heretofore-opposing portions of the body to get involved, indeed to partner as one body with acts of service. Such activities bring differing parts of the Kingdom together to accomplish great deeds. Yeshua is not coming back until He sees His church performing His will for His purposes.

Kindly consider the bride's appearance. She is dressed in fine linen. This same material is assigned to the priests who ministered at the Temple. God instructed those who approached His throne to be clean. Linen was worn out of reverence for God and in obedience to His instructions for priestly garb. The clothing was white, symbolizing purity and holiness. And this is not just any material, this is fine linen, referred to in Leviticus 16:4 as *"holy garments."*

Pharaoh clothed Joseph in linen. The ephod, the breastplate of righteousness worn by Samuel, was made of fine woven linen. David danced before the Lord in fine linen. Mordecai wore linen as an expression of the king's gratitude. Esther decorated her courts in linen. God told Jeremiah to put a linen sash around his waist. Angelic hosts in Ezekiel's vision wore linen. Daniel envisioned a man clothed in linen. Note that the curtains of the tabernacle were constructed of fine woven linen.

Priestly garments required fine linen tunic, sash, and trousers. Linen was used to form the hem of the priestly robe holding bells of pure gold, alternating with images of pomegranates. Naturally we are reminded of the woman with the issue of blood who grabbed the hem of Yeshua's robe in an act of faith. And last, the body of Jesus was wrapped in linen as His burial garment.

Then the astounding revelation—the fine linen *"is the righteous acts of the saints."* The bride of our King is clothed in service. Not just prayer or worship. Not just sacrificial giving of tithes and offerings. The Lord our God wants to know if we are fulfilling the mission and ministry He has called His saints to perform. He is not looking for the best doctrine. He does not expect a fancy dress. God longs to see His church poured out in lovingkindness to a dying world. That is beautiful to our God.

To be clothed in Christ is to be clothed in righteousness. Such awareness leads us to touch a world that hungers for wholeness and oneness with God. This is the image of God that He planted within each of us before the foundation of the earth. Our desire for righteousness is our supernaturally implanted seed of faith that spurs us on to do good works, while we await the call of our Betrothed.

Use your talents. Fill your jars with oil. Cast your nets. Do righteous acts.

When Yeshua returns for His bride, He will be looking for the woman described in Revelation 19:6-7:

> *And I heard, as it were, the voice of a great multitude, as the sound of many waters and as the sound of mighty thunderings, saying, "Alleluia! For the Lord God Omnipotent reigns! Let us be glad and rejoice and give Him glory, for the marriage of the Lamb has come, and His wife has made herself ready."*

The sound of Heaven's great multitude sounds like many waters. Living water is what flows from the throne of God. Water is the place where Jesus teaches us how to fish. Water is the place where we are immersed. Water is the place of shelter within the mother's womb. Water is the substance through which God shed His light in creation.

Revelation 19 directs us to listen to Heaven. The voices of the angelic hosts are singing and praising God over and over. As they praise they repeat the word, "Alleluia!"

"Alleluia!" appears four times in the first six verses of Revelation chapter 19. This is the only time this illustrious word is used in all of the Holy Scriptures.

Hine! Listen! Over and over again Heaven exults. Each exultation is followed by an exclamation point. The outcry of worship voiced is "Alleluia!" as the saints proclaim the living God.

The River of God Is Full

Psalm 65 reminds us the River of God is full of water. In our opening scenario recall the steady flow right next to the ponds. There is ample depth, lots of fish, and plenty of provision in the moving stream. The arm of the Lord is never too short to save us from our own problems as well as those of others.

Looking beyond the wind and beneath the waves, Yeshua shows us He has mastery over all the elements. He stills the tempest. But if we are going to walk on the water, we will have to overcome those temptations that will drown us. This is more than stepping out of the boat; this is a leap of faith.

On the surface, the distractions of life appear to be overpowering. Without an abiding relationship with God, we won't look for ways to walk on the water. The typical response to wind and rain is to seek shelter from the storm. Nor did Yeshua teach us to hold our nose and submerge ourselves into the sea to avoid the conflict around us. The gospel is not designed to separate us from life's issues. God gives us His Word to gain a heavenly worldview on our predicament. That perspective tells us that, unless we keep our eyes firmly fixed upon Yeshua, we're all wet.

Peter was not able to walk on the water without embracing the person of Yeshua—the one whom God sent. Peter made a conscious choice to follow God. If we make any attempt at self-protection, it changes our motives. Once our motives shift from honoring the King, our own agenda becomes more important than His. Peter sank the moment he took his eyes off of Yeshua. It's no different for you and me. Even if I think I've got it all together and I can walk on water, the mildest distraction means I will join the fish below.

Something happened to us. Something was unleashed in the Garden of Eden. Something hungered for greater status and higher standing among our peers. There came a desire for recognition. We wanted to know how it feels to run the show. In layman's terms, we were getting too big for our britches. We wanted forbidden fruit.

It wasn't enough to be fed and humbled by what we had received from God. When sin entered, it justified our taking instead of our giving. A life of celebrity became our highest goal. Thankfully, by the grace of God, there is only one celebrity in the Kingdom of Heaven, and that's Yeshua.

He showed us how to live a life of humility by laying down all the power and authority given to Him. He was sitting on the right hand of Yahweh. He was in the highest place anyone could ever imagine achieving. And He laid it all down for you and for me. That decision shattered every possible excuse for us to be superstars.

Worldly success actually challenges our own ability to discover our true identity. We may be rewarded for achieving or practicing something that brings us great recognition or material compensation, but such success can deter us from drawing near to God. Then, faith in God is replaced by faith in ourselves or by placing our trust in some outside authority that claims to have our best interests at heart.

Everything will be tested. Only those things that honor God can withstand close scrutiny. Saint Peter walked on water because he had faith in God, not because of any inherent ability. In fact, Peter had some of the best fishing credentials in all of Galilee.

Nevertheless, he repeatedly failed to maintain his most passionate promises—those he made face to face with Jesus. Once Peter followed Yeshua's directive to get out of the boat and walk on water, he broadcasts to all humanity that a fully committed child of God could enter into the supernatural realm while on earth.

Nothing has changed since that day when Yeshua released Peter to walk on the water. God's ability to lift us into His Majestic Glory while we are still living and breathing on earth has not diminished one jot or tittle. If our fears overcome us, His hand is quick to grab us and put us back in the boat, so we can go fishing again.

Weigh Anchor

The River of Life flows from beneath the Temple in Ezekiel's vision. Drink in the image the prophet shares with us. This river flows freely from the throne of God all the way to the Dead Sea. There is abundance and multiplicity of life. Creatures will gather to be renewed. Fishermen are drawn for a great catch of fish. A variety of trees will bear fruit. The waters have the capacity to restore and refresh and to heal, because they flow from the Sanctuary of God.

> *He said to me, "Have you seen this, son of man?" Then he brought me back to the bank of the river. When I had returned, behold, there were very many trees on each side and on the other, along the bank of the river. Then he said to me, "These waters go out toward the eastern region. They go down to the Arabah and enter the sea. When they arrive at the sea,* **the waters of the sea will flow and will become fresh. It will be that every living creature that swarms will live wherever the rivers go. There will be a very great multitude of fish**, *because this water goes there and makes the salt water fresh. So* **everything will be healed and live wherever the river goes. Fishermen will stand by it;** *from En-gedi to En-eglaim, it will be a place for spreading of nets.* **Their fish will be of many different kinds**—*like the fish of the Great Sea, a huge quantity. Its swamps and marshes will not become fresh; they will be set aside for salt.* **On the river, on its bank, on this side and that side, will grow every kind**

of tree for food. Its leaf will not wither; its fruit will not fail; it will bear new fruit every month, because its water flows from out from the Sanctuary. Its fruit will be for food and its leaf will be for healing" (Chapter 47:6-12 TLV).

Our God wants us to be healed and fed directly from His River. There is no other source that can provide the gifts of God. He is complete and His heart is for us to be complete in Him.

To be fishers of men is to, "Go!" where God asks us to go. Only then will we experience the abundance God has in store for us.

May your nets be ever full.

Shalom.

Noteworthy Ketches*

*A ketch is a fishing boat in the traditional sense. In the context of this book, the following ketches are organizations that are reaching out to meet people's needs with the love of God and "catching fish" who are hungry for the Good News. May these models inspire you to build your own fishing boat, climb aboard one of the ministries mentioned, or seek ones that may already be casting nets in your locale.

Neighborhood Initiative

Neighborhood Initiative is the body of Christ at work in neighborhoods where God has placed us to bring about the transformation that comes through the power of His Kingdom. Neighborhood Initiative is *not* a program, it is a work that God is introducing to bring revival in His church and transformation to our cities. It's an organization encouraging people to go out into their own neighborhoods to befriend their neighbors, open their homes, and lend a hand.

From the About Us website page: In January of 2001, some of the pastors from the west valley of Los Angeles began gathering to pray for our city and the churches that make up the whole church in our valley. It was our commitment from the beginning to pray, to develop relationships with one another, and to wait on the Lord to show us what He had in mind for us to do. The Lord made it apparent that He was leading us to minister together in the neighborhoods where those in our churches live. This ministry has become known as Neighborhood Initiative. Resources are available for pastors and leaders interested in implementing their own neighborhood initiative in their cities. Check out our Neighboring Resources to get started! There is also a leaders and participants guide available for pastors who want to use these materials in their own churches. Visit Resources/Neighboring Resources.
Neighborhood Initiative motto:

the WHOLE church
taking the WHOLE gospel
to the WHOLE city
one neighborhood at a time

Contact information:
Website: http://neighborhoodinitiative.com/
lynncory@neighborhoodinitiative.org
Neighborhood Initiative
6642 Reseda Blvd, Reseda, CA 91335
Phone: 818-269-3608

Rotary Club

The Rotary Club's efforts to eradicate polio have been described as one of the finest humanitarian projects the world has ever known, and the Rotary Club has even been nominated for the Nobel Peace Prize. When the club's goal has been completed, the eradication of polio will be one of the most significant achievements in public health since the elimination of smallpox.

Thirty years ago polio was an epidemic that struck mercilessly around the world. In the 1980s, one thousand new cases a day were reported. Currently only three countries in the world have yet to stop the transmission of the poliovirus: Afghanistan, Nigeria, and Pakistan. Last year less than 370 cases were confirmed in the world. This represents over a 99 percent reduction of illness.

Rotary partners with other organizations, multiplying the impact of their efforts. From local food banks to global humanitarian organizations, they know the power that comes from uniting.

Contact information:

Website: https://www.rotary.org
Rotary International
One Rotary Center
1560 Sherman Ave.
Evanston, IL 60201-3698
Phone: 866-976-8279 (toll free)

Kingdom Life Community Association

A Korean man decides the church needs to tear down walls of separation between the Latin and Latino communities. He sponsors breakfasts twice a year, along with an annual conference, to inform church leaders about God's plan for unity. These meetings now draw close to 150 pastors. Except now, people of every race attend. At these gatherings speakers promote the vision of the one new man and assist one another to advance the Kingdom of God in Los Angeles.

From the Message from President Website page:

I believe that the love of Jesus Christ is able to bring us together in unity. In 1992, the rifts in our society created by years of economic and racial disparities developed into the "Perfect Storm" that brought violence and destruction to our streets giving birth to the LA Riots. Many have studied the incident and wrote reports on what could be improved to prevent such an event in the future. And since then, Los Angeles has seen the birth of many community organizations which focus on the political and social power of their respective ethnic groups. However, even now, our society has not developed solutions for potential conflict and the racial tension that exists between different ethnic groups. Why? It is because of our sin. As we know, Jesus is the answer…as Christian leaders and pastors, we can be the ideal role models for our respective communities and overcome any differences and disagreements that may exist, and work together to build a true community of faith, continuing the Ministry of Reconciliation, not only between us and God, but with each other.

Kingdom Living Community Association

Contact information:

Website: http://klca4christ.org
Kingdom Living Community Association
981 S. Western Ave. Suite 202
Los Angeles, CA 90005
Telephone: 323-600-5672

CARE 18 Presents FIAT

CARE 18 stands for Communication, Advocacy, Recovery, Engagement. Their website says, "An 18-month initial project to address human trafficking of minors in Los Angeles with a victim-centered approach and a focus on safe housing and wrap-around services."

Their brochure says, "Los Angeles has one of the highest rates of human trafficking of any city in the US." Here's a proactive group that is gathering representatives from business, civic, and faith-based organizations to tackle a tragic, deeply ingrained problem.

FIAT (Faith Initiative Against Trafficking) is a gathering of churches and individuals who have been called to fight human trafficking. They train and encourage believers to get actively involved in confronting slavery.

Website: http://www.care18.org

HBN—Hosanna Broadcasting Network

HBN calls itself, "The Voice of Jesus Christ." Run by an Ethiopian woman, this dynamic network broadcasts a strong gospel message via television across the United States and via radio to the Middle East and parts of Africa and Asia. The network also boasts a foundation that houses 20 orphaned girls in Addis Abba, the capitol of Ethiopia. Recognizing that just a small fraction of their audience even owns a television, this network delivers the Word of God on satellite radio to an unreached part of the world. They also televise a straight gospel message on satellite to North America.

From the website: It is our desire to bring change in lives of people who are in need whether in underserved areas or in metropolitan cities. We are committed to set a new standard in media. We are also about empowering lives of the communities we serve, therefore we implement programs locally or internationally that will contribute to the welfare of children and youth.

Contact information:

Hosanna Broadcasting Network
3711 N. Long Beach Blvd. Suite 5044
Long Beach, CA 90807
Office Ph. 562-247-0409
Cell 562-208-5303
http://www.hosannabroadcasting.com

The Kingdom Center

I stood in the parking lot crying. An old motel that had once been the center of crime, prostitution, and drug dealers for Ventura, California, surrounded me. There is a plaque by each door with the name of a church inscribed—22 different churches in all. Every church had adopted a homeless family right off the streets. These families are housed in completely refurbished rooms. New carpet, tile, plumbing, and paint. There are bunk beds and a playground for kids… Social services oversaw counseling and job applications. The church was unified.

From the website: The Kingdom Center Oxnard, an adjacent community, began when a city council member from Oxnard saw what was going on to provide love, acceptance, and provision at The Kingdom Center Ventura and called Pastor Sam Gallucci. We have been called to do through unity with the churches in Oxnard and Ventura County to minister to "the least of these among us." The mission of The Kingdom Center is to unite churches, businesses, and individuals to provide transitional housing to homeless families so they can lead productive and happy lives in our community. Our vision is that we can come together as a community to provide hope, resources and strength to those less fortunate, empowering them to become productive members of our community.

Contact information:
Website: http://tkcoxnard.org
info@tkcoxnard.org
The Kingdom Center Oxnard
PO Box 654
Oxnard, CA 93032
Telephone: 805-487-3400

Navajo Israel Agricultural Gathering

On stage were four Israeli agricultural experts. They had traveled halfway around the planet to teach the First Nations how to turn their desert into a garden, just as they had done in the Holy Land. The auditorium was filled with Native Americans, Hispanics, Anglos, and locals from around Shiprock, New Mexico. The Holy Scriptures were being fulfilled. The Navajos had honored Israel during their journey to Jerusalem the previous year. Now Israel was returning the blessing.

I will never forget the day of our first conference in Farmington, New Mexico, when Pastor Tso informed me that his fellow people had told him, "We have been waiting for the Jews to come." I wondered how long had that hope been hidden in the hearts of the oppressed. And here we stood as the dream was being played out in front of us. What a privilege.

I would encourage all who wish to advance the Kingdom of God to look around the neighborhood where you live. Find a partner or two or more. There is so much we can do. Our Lord so wants to bless us as we carry His glory into our communities. Far too many of us sit on the threshold of greatness. For example, there are more than 500 First Nations in America. Discover which are near you. They've been given spiritual authority over this land. Many can use your help. Jump in the river! The water's fine.

Kehilat HaCarmel – The Assembly on Mount Carmel

We were standing on Holy Ground, on the high place of Mount Carmel. This was most likely the exact site where Elijah called down fire on his water-drenched sacrifice. High praise and worship were going up to Heaven as a pleasing aroma to our King. Christians and Jews, Arabs and Hebrews, Palestinians and Israelis were all worshipping Yeshua the Messiah together. Hallelujah! After the service we hugged one another as *mishpocha* (Hebrew for relatives by blood, marriage, and close friendship). I was seeing what the peace of God looked like when everyone worshipped the Messiah of Israel in one accord. What man thought was impossible had been accomplished by our mighty God!

From the website: Kehilat HaCarmel is a community of Messianic believers located on Mt. Carmel in the city of Haifa. Rebuilding God's altar in Israel today means bringing the "living stones" of God's people together—Jews, Arabs, and other Gentiles being forged into "one new man" in the fire of His love.

Contact information:
Website: http://www.carmel-assembly.org.il/#
info@carmel-assembly.org.il
Kehilat HaCarmel
PO Box 7004
Haifa, 31070
Israel
972-4-839-1347

Fishing

There's a change in the wind of the Holy Spirit. Can you feel it?
A fresh scent fills the air. A quickening summons all hands on deck.
The alarm has sounded. Senses alerted.
Salty spray anoints calloused hands.
Eager eyes scrutinize emerging horizons.
Morning mist shrouds distant shores.
Crisscrossing currents tucked under liquid lanes mark our progress in cadenced lapping against the hull.

We wonder, "Will the catch gather where once we swept our nets?
Surely they seek a more secure haven."
Sails strain to gather galloping gusts.
Taut lines tug against rusted cleats,
Stretching to contain the expansive release of Heaven's hosts.
Frothy foam outlines lips of surging surf.
Our bow slices wind-whipped waves, cutting a heading toward dawn.
Canvas sighs and swells, inhaling, embracing formless forces.

Rushing. Rushing. Pushing past pain.
Nothing remains but purpose.
Voices of angels penetrate the atmosphere. Harkening. Harkening.
Whispering wishes of warriors who spent their all.
The Spirit says to the Church, "You have reached your reward."

Blurred forearms splay nets.
Unleashed, they descend 'neath the vessel's shadowy stern.
Fishers of men prepare to haul. Anticipation arises.

Muscly sinews draw crusty cords.
Capturing hidden treasures that once called these darkened depths home.
Up comes the web breaching, disrupting the opaque, glassy surface.
Alas! Silvery scales reflect glistening brightness.
The catch gasps for its watery estate.
Striving to survive—not knowing the freedom of salvation on the other side.

Then choosing to die, that others be released.

Our past perfected by sinless sacrifice.
Our present illuminated with the hope of His calling.
Our destiny assured by blood. Our course plotted in ages past.

No turning back now.
Fishing—just keep fishing.

www.ingramcontent.com/pod-product-compliance
Lightning Source LLC
Chambersburg PA
CBHW071729080526
44588CB00013B/1954